D1548435

50 Cent:

No Holds Barred

by Jake Brown

Colossus Books

Phoenix
New York   Los Angeles

THE AMAZING TRUE STORY OF A BLACK TEEN WHO DEFIED THE ODDS DID JAIL TIME   ESCAPED THE HOOD

BECAME AN INTERNATIONALLY-RENOWNED AWARD WINNING GANGSTA RAPPER AND MULTI-MILLIONAIRE

50 defied all the odds, and with no holds barred, put the rap game in a much-needed choke hold that has brought authenticity back to the forefront as a goal for all of his peers to shoot for, as long as they aren't aiming at 50, because his armor includes bullet-proof vests, bling bling, and layers & layers of platinum.

After years of struggle, 50 Cent's perseverance is finally paying off, BIG TIME!

Get Rich Or Die Tryin'!!!!!

SHOCKING!!   RIVETING!!   INTENSE!!

Vividly describes 50 Cents' obstacles and victories as a rapper.
—Source Magazine

50 got shot 9 times...and... he ain't going anywhere.

50 Cent:

No Holds Barred

by Jake Brown

Colossus Books

Phoenix
New York   Los Angeles

50 Cent: No Holds Barred
by Jake Brown

Published by:
Colossus Books
A Division of Amber Communications Group, Inc.
1334 East Chandler Boulevard, Suite 5-D67
Phoenix, Z 85048
amberbk@aol.com
WWW.AMBERBOOKS.COM

Tony Rose, Publisher/Editorial Director   Samuel P. Peabody, Associate Publisher
Yvonne Rose, Senior Editor   The Printed Page, Interior & Cover Design

Library of Congress
Catalog-in-Publication Information Pending
Library of Congress Cataloging-in-Publication Data

Brown, Jake
  50 Cent : no holds barred / by Jake Brown.
    p. cm.
  ISBN 0-9767735-2-X (pbk. : alk. paper) 1. 50 Cent (Musician) 2. Rap musicians—United States—Biography. I. Title.
  ML420.A02B76 2005
  782.421649'092—dc22

                                                        2005043667

Contents

Dedicated to my Alison and Bri,

With Love and Promise, Jake, August, 2004

About the Author

Jake Brown resides in Nashville, Tennessee and is President of Versailles Records. An avid writer he has penned several books, including the best-sellers: *SUGE KNIGHT – The Rise, Fall & Rise of Death Row Records; Your Body's Calling Me: The Life and Times of Robert "R" Kelly – Music Love, Sex & Money and READY to Die: The Story of Biggie —Notorious B.I.G.* Upcoming titles on Colossus Books are: *Jay-Z. …AND the Roc-A-Fella Dynasty and Tupac SHAKUR (2-PAC) IN the Studio: The Studio Years (1987-1996).*

"I got my back against the wind,
I'm down to ride till the sun burns out
If I die today, I'm happy how my life turned out
See the shootouts that I've been in, I'm by myself
Locked up I was in a box by myself
I done made myself a millionaire by myself..."

—*50 Cent—Heat, 2003*

Prologue

After years of struggle, 50 Cent's perseverance is finally paying off, BIG TIME, such that less than a year after the release of his debut LP, 50, in October, 2003, moved out of his native Queens, New York neighborhood for good and into a 52-room mansion in Farmington, Connecticut, formally owned by boxer Mike Tyson.

An opulent celebration of the fruits of 50's labors, the house stands as a true testament to 50's achievement as the millennium's first true hip hop superstar, the rapper admitted that when he's not onstage, "I like to spend time in the house regular just relaxing, because I do so much moving around yanno. I got a nice house but I don't have a chance to stay in it much."

Boasting 18 bedrooms, 25 full baths, an elevator, 2 billiard rooms, a movie theatre, full gym and locker room, and an elevator, the house spans 50,000 square feet and cost the rapper $4.1 million.

In the house's massive garage, 50 parks a extensive collection of top-line luxury automobiles, including a Lamborghini, a Mercedes SL500, a BMW 745I, an H2, and a custom-made bullet and bomb-proof Chevy Suburban, which 50 jokes you could "throw a stick of dynamite at...and it'd probably be alright."

50 appeared to be so comfortable in his new digs that he even toyed with running for Town Council, according to staff writer Bill Larkin of The Herald of New Britain, 50's local town newspaper, who enthusiastically endorsed what most feel was a very light-hearted joke on the rapper's part, arguing in an editorial that "the rapper's term in office would add much-needed diversity to a council consisting solely of older Caucasian men."

Avoiding politics for the time being, ensuring a better life for his son Marquise seems to be 50's top priority, as he also used some of his new found wealth to set up a $10 million life insurance policy for his only child in 2003. 50 clearly seems to realize his position as a role model first with his own child. Therein, the rapper appears to prefer to use that relationship as an archetype for how he then preaches outward to fans' parents or fans with children who also might be exposed to his music and the reality of its inherently violent content.

As such, while 50 has gone to great lengths to let his son know that 'daddy's reality will never be yours', the rapper in the same time doesn't try to shelter his son from the existence of that reality. Clearly, 50 feels his boy will have a greater appreciation for what he has materially knowing where his father came from, and what he went through to provide that security for his son.

The rapper also seems to recommend this approach to his fans who do not come from the inner city, namely the suburban demographic, either as listeners or with children who are fans, explaining that "(my son) knows what's going on...I explained it to him exactly how (listeners) gonna have to explain it to their kids when they hear my music. You see, if your kid is listening to my music, you need to sit him down and explain to him that some peoples lives is like TV—(but, by contrast) the shots do go off in the hood. People do get hit. (But) if that's not actually the life surrounding (your) kid, you can (still) let that kid (know) that that's what really goes on in certain places cuz that be goin on in my real life situations."

Expanding on the aforementioned, while 50 clearly wants a better life for his own boy, he makes a point of teaching his son an appreciation for the contrast between what he has and what 50 had to do to provide it by keeping him in the loop on his own past, even those portions that some parents might want to keep their children sheltered from completely, explaining candidly that "(my son) understands what's going on even though he's only 6 years old. He knows exactly what's goin on. When he sees me put my (bulletproof) vest on before I leave the house, he asks me do I have my vest sometimes. I set it around (in the open). My son asked 'Daddy, why you carry a gun, you ain't a cop?' I looked at him, and said 'Sometimes you gotta shot or be shot.'"

"It is what it is. I don't try to sugar coat it or nothing (because he'll get it easier that way). I try to explain (to) him that I'm blessed, and in a situation (where) I can provide another situation for him so he don't have to go through that. The only reason I took him to shoot the 'Wanksta' video is I wanted to show him there was other things out there (in the world and hood) to do, outside of what's goin on right (in his immediate world). To me that's it...(Its sad sometimes because) I don't spend much time with my son 'cause I'm traveling. I don't pay child support from no court telling me I have to pay child support, I support them 'cause that's my son's mother and that's my son. I'll just take care of him financially and make sure his school and everything is set up proper. But to be honest with you, I'm running around (so I don't see him much)."

50's matter-of-fact outlook on life is rooted completely in reality, which is refreshing in a millennium where reality rap has largely become a character of itself. In terms of keeping it real both with his own child and with his fans, 50 makes no apologies, and offering only honesty about what he did to reach the remarkable pinnacle he has attained at 28 years of age, almost a decade removed from his prison sentence for crack dealing, and a lifetime from where society statistically expected him to end up.

50 defied all the odds, and with *no holds barred*, put the rap game in a much-needed choke hold that has brought authenticity back to the forefront as a goal for all of his peers to shoot for, as long as they aren't aiming at 50, because his armor includes bullet-proof vests, bling bling, and layers and layers of platinum. As far as he has come in his short but remarkable lifetime, 50 has already attained the status of a living legend, but remains markedly grounded, always in touch with the streets that made him, and almost took his life from him.

By never forgetting where he came from, 50 is able to stay acutely aware of what lays ahead of him, both in terms of danger, and the promise of even greater glory, "I hustled, that's the only way I could get what I wanted, because the other way was too hard. I can't do it that way. I dropped out (of school), I'm hustlin' man. I'm not doin' good at (school, because) everything is not for everybody."

"They could say whatever, (but) I ended up getting my GED in the joint, in jail. But if I wasn't in jail, I wouldn't have gotten it cuz I would've been out in the street...Since I got shot, I don't get worked up about things that are out of my control...You get shot 9 times, you feel like you here for a reason, especially when the guy shooting you is as close as you and, you gotta feel you here for a reason...I ain't going anywhere. I feel like I have the same chance of living to 40 as anybody else in New York City."

Gotta Make It To Heaven

50 Cent and the Rebirth
of the Spirit of Tupac in Hip Hop

Hip-hop's biggest selling point has always been authenticity. Whether inherently a part of an MC's character, or an earned attribute in the course of developing a professional persona, rappers have always had to live up to a certain expectation of criminality that equaled the lifestyle outlined in their rhymes, at the very least as part of their background. They need not always be a true living incarnation of their professional personality, though it never hurt album sales if they did.

Fans related more directly to a rapper if, for example, a rapper had a verifiable criminal record, the more recent and colorful the better. Either because the listener could relate to the MC's struggles as a mirror of their own life in the case of an inner city listener, or as an escape from a more monotonous every day existence, usually among rap's suburban audience. Regardless, the presence of a criminal record greatly enhanced the sales of that very thing at retail.

The best illustration of the latter formula in action is found in the short but epic life of late hip hop legend Tupac Shakur, who had no rap sheet prior to beginning his career, but quickly racked up real life convictions that qualified the persona he played out on his records as he rose rapidly to the pinnacle of hip hop popularity among fans around the world. Tupac lived fast and died young, literally, and he was beloved for it. His fans felt he rode for them like no hip hop MC ever had before, and his topical versatility allowed him to appeal to virtually every sect of hip hop's total audience.

Tupac also was the first MC to authenticate himself in real time—if he rapped about shoot outs with the police, you could read about it in the papers within the next day. If he rapped about growing up around the systematic oppression of his people, one need look no further than his mother, Black Panther Afeni Shakur, who had given birth to Tupac in prison while on trial for conspiracy to blow up a federal building in the early 1970s.

If Tupac rapped about being shot, you could point to the robbery-shooting that put 5 shots in his body and almost took his life. If he rapped about being locked down, fans could look to his 11 month lockdown in Clinton Correctional Facility in upstate New York between 1994 and 1995 before Suge Knight bailed him out by posting $1.4 million in bail. Thereafter, if Tupac rapped about being out on bail, he literally was. Perhaps most potent among his rhyming arsenal was Tupac's prophetic statement—a recurring theme over and over in his raps—that he would die in the statistical vein of the young, black male that he so consummately embodied.

Therein, when he did, tragically, in the fall of 1996, fans were saddened, but Tupac had prepared them for it, and his spirit of survival lifted rap up collectively to move on. Shakur set the bar for hip hop as a commercial entity, showing corporate America what rappers were capable of in terms of record sales, generating $80 Million in the last year of his life and career for Death Row Records and its distributor, Interscope. As an inspiration not only to millions of America's hip hop listeners, but also to an entirely new generation of aspiring MCs looking not to eclipse Tupac's influence in hip hop, only perhaps to equal it.

As rap's Michael Jordan, Tupac was its universal propheteer, breaking down all barriers, and setting himself apart on virtually every level of achievement available to a superstar MC. Since his demise, only one MC, aside from possibly Jay-Z, has emerged as a potential heir, a Queens-born rapper who has drawn more natural comparisons to Tupac than any other MC to emerge since Shakur's demise in 1996.

A wordsmith who, perhaps mutually out of respect and ambition, aspired in his first hit single for fans 'to love me like they love Pac.' His name is Curtis Jackson, better known to the world as 50 Cent, and many feel he could be the next life of Tupac, at least in spirit and mass appeal. The surface comparisons are eerie—from their natural charisma as stars to their prolific ability to record and release records to the similarity in their beefs with fellow rap stars to the fact that both were shot multiple times and survived, at least the first time.

Most believe there will not be another 50 Cent, just as the industry knew instantly there would never be another Tupac, even before we lost him. Perhaps one of the only differences between the two men, in terms of generic comparisons, is that 50 plans to hang around a while longer. A listener can identify optimism in his music—however cautious, while Tupac made it common knowledge that he expected to die young.

With that in mind, Shakur set out to make history, recording roughly 150 songs in the 8 months between his release from prison in 1995 and demise in 1996, the results being 7 posthumous albums to date, including 3 double-albums and 2 single discs of previously unreleased material, as well as a two-disc greatest hits collection, and soundtrack album. That's an average of an album a year for the 8 years he has been deceased. 50 Cent has demonstrated a similar work ethic out of the gate, releasing a debut album, which sold 7 million copies, a group LP, and a DVD featuring 6 new songs, all in the first year of his career in 2003.

This impressive catalog makes no mention of his multiple 'street' releases via mixtape in the years leading up to his signing with Eminem's Shady Records in 2002. Throughout 2003, 50 Cent continued to show up on mix tapes even after he was a bona fide mainstream star, and his sophomore album is expected in late 2004. All told, 50 Cent has sold 12 million records in his first year, grossed $18 million personally, written a biography and begun production on a movie partially based on his life story.

As his professional blueprint largely appears to mirror Tupac's, so too does his personal upbringing upon examination in many respects. While Shakur grew up raised by a single-mother, 50 Cent lost his own in a drug-deal gone wrong at the age of 9—both women at one time were crack addicts. Both grew up in the inner city ghettos of the East Coast, 50 Cent in Queens, New York, Shakur in both New York and Baltimore till his mid-teens.

While Shakur would begin racking up criminal convictions as his career took off, 50 Cent was a drug dealer throughout his teens, authenticated by convictions for heroine possession and intent to distribute. Both men faced incarceration—Shakur later in his career for a sexual assault conviction, while 50 spent time in an upstate New York prison for his aforementioned drug peddling convictions.

Both men were also almost murdered at one point in their young lives because of their authentic involvement in the seedier side of hip hop's criminal affiliation, Shakur 5 times and 50 Cent 9 times respectively, whereafter both miraculously survived. While the stories of their professional discovery differ, their lives naturally mirror one another's in enough substantial manners to wonder whether it is coincidence, or a reflection of the fact that both MCs were put on this earth to be superstars, to influence and change the world in their own manners, with Shakur serving as something of an acknowledged mentor to 50 Cent.

Professionally, both rappers owe some of their biggest hits to rap super-producer Dr. Dre, who also served as label-boss to Shakur and 50 Cent at different times in each other's career, and whose presence helped to propel both rappers into hip hop's upper stratosphere of superstardom. Despite his countless comparisons to Shakur, 50 Cent in no way is a knock off. His most distinctive comparison to Shakur is in fact his originality, which was first discovered by legendary Run DMC DJ Jam Master Jay back in 1996, the same year that Tupac was taken from the world. The same year Curtis Jackson as a rapper was born into it.

While he would go through a faulty deal with (Atlantic Records) which would end at the time his life almost did, 50 Cent would continue his climb out of the ghetto between 1999 and 2002—seemingly via the old fashioned way, but in reality as one of the pioneers of what has become the hottest new trend in hip hop—the mix tape.

At one time mix tapes were a vehicle for underground rappers to establish a buzz on the street before being discovered and eventually signed to a major label. However, that process, due to the runaway phenomenon mix tapes have become, largely due to 50 Cent's success, has reversed itself overnight, now operating as a booming bootleg industry wherein established rap stars seek out underground DJs in the hopes of appearing on whatever the hottest new mix tape release will be. This is done in part to keep themselves fresh with the newest inner-city hip hop listeners, but also because of the fact that mix tapes have brought hip hop back down to a street level of authenticity it had grown away from in the years since the demise of Tupac Shakur.

This evolution was natural in the course of hip hop becoming a billion dollar industry in the latter half of the 1990s, but the majority of hip hop's superstars also got swept away in all the limelight, and fans in effect lost touch with hip hop's root authenticity as the genre became mainstream music's strongest seller.

The void is not an obvious one, but with the many tangent industries that bloomed out of rap's commercial crossover—popular examples including movies, clothing lines and related product endorsements—many of hip hop's more experienced listeners, who had been rescued in the early 1990s by Death Row Records with Tupac Shakur and Bad Boy Entertainment with the Notorious BIG from the saturation of New Jack, were now being watered down and over commercialized a second time around.

Tupac's posthumous releases continued to sell in multi-platinum volume, but this was based on an established fan base and legacy. By the millennium, fans were hungry again for something raw and gleaming only in the rough. They found it with 50 Cent, who made himself hip hop's hottest underground commodity via mix tapes in the late 1990s and early years following 2000 before being discovered by rap's other millennium superstar, Eminem.

Because of the immediate media and fan attention on a mainstream level that accompanied 50 Cent's Million Dollar signing (literally) to a joint venture between Eminem's label, Shady Records, and Dr. Dre's parent label, Aftermath Entertainment, co-owned by Interscope Records, mix tapes suddenly became the both the most viable A&R tool and career resuscitation method for established rappers looking to reinvent themselves in hip hop's ever-changing and evolving marketplace.

50 Cent has proven to be a literal wheel of reinvention for hip hop, and as a new century dawns, he shows no signs of slowing down. Quite literally he is just getting started, still because of what he has survived personally and accomplished professionally, there already is a compelling story to be told. Here's how it began...

Chapter 1
Curtis James Jackson III

50 Cent was born Curtis James Jackson III was born on July 6th, 1976, in the inner-city New York neighborhood of South Jamaica, in the borough of Queens. In many ways, 50 Cent was born a statistic, like millions of fellow inner city young black males, his father was absent from the rapper's world from the time of 50's first breath out of the womb.

His mother, Sabrina Jackson, still in many ways a child herself by definition, was just 15 at the time of her son's birth, and would be dead within 8 years, at the age of 23. 50 remembers his mother as "real aggressive. My mom used to like women. I think she had a girlfriend when I was eight years old. She was really manly, really tough, and she had to be—she was hustling. I spent a lot of time with my grandmother even before my mother passed."

Surprisingly or not, 50's mother was herself a drug dealer, years before 50 was, although its not clear whether the circumstances of her murder were related to her profession, "She was dead for days before they found her. When they found her, her body was fucked-up. Someone put something in her drink and turned the gas on."

Concerning 50's feelings for his mother's profession, he saw it through the same lens of logic as he did his own decision to deal drugs as a young teen, such that "twenty-eight years ago, having a teen pregnancy wasn't as common as it is these days. When it happened, she started to hustle to provide for me. You know? And...she,

1

she got killed. And after she got killed, I stayed with my grandparents."

According to the rapper, he recalled his grandmother, who he had stayed with off and on in the years preceding his mother's murder, breaking the news of his mother's death to him as simply as possible, such that "my Grandmother and them told me 'Your mother's not coming home. She's not gonna come back to pick you up. You're gonna stay with us now.'…But (my mom) was in the streets so much, I'd stayed with (my grandparents) before, too."

In terms of when 50 found out about the specific cause of his mother's death, he explained that his Grandmother broke it too him years later, partly the rapper implies, because she wanted to shelter him from the harshness of the circumstances. Additionally, however, 50 surmises his Grandmother kept the details from him because she was personally uncomfortable with sharing his mother's sexual orientation with the young child, a decision he suggests was motivated in part by his Grandmother's personal disapproval of her daughter's lifestyle choices in that area, "I got (the details of) what happened (to my mom) later."

"My grandmother was uncomfortable even saying that my mother liked girls." The rapper himself has chosen, in later years, to stay as neutral as possible on the subject of alternative lifestyles, explaining that, from his vantage point, his mother was not categorically a "lesbian. I don't know what you call it—bisexual? I'm here, so it had to be bi. But I think that's why I don't pass judgment on people."

Following his mother's murder, 50 was raised in a very religious household, essentially adopted by his Grandparents, such that today, he considers himself the product of a loving household, despite the fact that both his parents were largely absent from his upbringing, "I was my grandmothers baby…She's special—she's been there the entire time…She's been the positive portion of my life the entire time."

Moreover, from 50's vantage point, even as a young child, it was more unusual for kids to grow up in a two-parent home than in a single-parent one, which worked to help him maintain a healthy, adjusted perspective on his own situation growing up without either of his parents, "in my neighborhood, if you had both parents, you were spoiled—'You got a mother and a father? Oh shit!'"

From that vantage point, it was likely easier to psychologically embrace his Grandparents as equal to what his parents would have been in the way of caretakers, had either been around during his formative years. One aspect of the way his Grandmother brought him up that 50 seems to appreciate to date is the fact that, according to the rapper, she never forced idealism on him, "She raised us Baptist, and when I got old enough to say I didn't want to go to church, she didn't force me. She was cool."

The latter is important as it relates to 50's exposure to the streets from such a young age in spite of the fact that he was the product of a loving home. 50 explains that it was the streets themselves, and perhaps his mother's history as a hustler, that drew his curiosity, rather than any neglect or abuse at home, which statistically pushes kids to rebel at that age, "(Once I'd gotten curious), I (still) had to be grandmother's little baby in the house, but I would be as aggressive as I had to be on the streets in order to (make my name out there)…"

"You could be in that neighborhood and not get in trouble, but trouble's there for you to get into. When you put people on top of people, it's that crabs-in-a-barrel theory. Rats in a box. Eventually they starve and start eating each other. Somebody's gonna take what you've got—unless you become the biggest problem. If you're not the biggest problem, you're in danger. When you're the biggest problem, there's nothing to fear, because everybody else is occupied with staying out of that zone. So the object is to be the biggest fucking problem in the neighborhood."

Still, out of respect for his Grandmother, he went out of his way to keep the two worlds as separate as possible, especially at the young age of 10 and 11, when 50 was first discovering his street persona. As he explained, "To a woman, (a polite kid) what you should be. I adjust to the situation. I had to be someone else when I was with my grandparents—I couldn't be who I was in the street when I went indoors, because I didn't want to disappoint them. I wouldn't curse in front of them. That's not acceptable." That etiquette has stayed with 50 to date out of respect for the job his Grandmother did raising him, "Even now that I'm grown I don't cuss in front of my Grandma."

The impact of his mother's death on the rapper at such a young age was clearly present in 50's conscience, especially as he got older and more aware of his mother's street reputation as a hustler. Still, while he seemed to pursue his interest over time in knowing more about his mother from an unsheltered street perspective, he explained that he had know competing interest in getting to know a thing about his father, who had abandoned him at birth. Clear in his mind, 50 was able to separate, and therein, reconcile within his own constitution, the reason for each of his parents' absence from his life growing up—in the case of his mother, it was helpless because of her murder.

Conversely, in the case of his father, whose absence was equally as senseless, to 50, the difference was his vacancy being intentional. In terms of the collective impact of the loss of his mother and father, keeping the respective circumstances behind their non-existence in mind, 50 has chosen to keep it completely real. Namely by being honest both with himself and his fans about how his father's abandoning him played into his own sense of value with regard to decisions he made growing up, the rapper is equally cognizant of the ways in which the latter balanced itself against the impact of his mother's absence—in terms of the choices 50 made growing up.

While some might argue that 50, in his younger years, displayed an uneven sense of self worth as he put his life on the line daily with his profession as a crack dealer (and almost lost it literally with the gang-style attempted murder on his life in his early 20s), as he got older, discovered his talent for rhyming, and specifically when his son was born, the rapper clearly began to develop a matured perspective on the value of human life, one he clearly keeps readily in mind when reflecting on his own lifestyle choices as they affect his role as a father, "I never knew my father, so I used losing her as an excuse. Every time something was wrong I'd think, if my mother was here, it wouldn't be like that."

"When I got shot, my son was in the house—so he heard me get shot. I'm sure it altered him. The average kid doesn't go through that." As much as he also adores and lives for being a good father to his son (reminiscent of Eminem and his daughter Hailey), 50 remains as uninterested as the latter rapper does in ever getting to know his birth father, explaining in terms both practical and personal terms that "I don't even want to meet him. I already missed the part where your father would be helpful. I'm a grown-assed man."

50's mother, in the early years of the rapper's life while she still alive and raising her son, explained his father's absence in sobering terms that reflected the realities of inner-city living, but, the rapper says, gave him a tangible way to interpret and live with the vacancy, feel good about himself as a person, and avoid feeling responsible in the process, "(My mother) told me I was born through immaculate conception: 'You don't have a father. You were born through Immaculate Conception, like Jesus.' It made me feel good not to have a father."

As 50 advanced into his elder pre-teen years, he became more and more curious about the streets his mother had come from. And while his Grandmother raised him in a loving environment at home, 50 tried to walk with a foot in each world, taking the encouragement he received domestically and turning it into motivation to be the best hustler he could be on the block, "My grandmother always told me just be the best. And I just figured out I wanted to be the best fuckin' bad guy. Im'ma do whatever the fuck I wanna do."

*"I'm alright, Nigga, I'm doing good
I ain't got to write rhymes, I got bricks in the hood."*

—50 Cent, "High All the Time"

Chapter 2
The Hustlin' Years —12-18

Drug dealing was essentially the family business to young Curtis Jackson, such that he followed in his mother's footsteps at age 12 when he first began selling crack. His motivation was a combination of curiosity, desire and eventually necessity. His mentors in the game understood the latter three for what they each represented as parts of a larger whole, the sum of which was all about money—both in terms of what it meant to principally have it in a neighborhood where there inherently was none, and also for the specific material things it could afford to give the poor kids growing up in that environment a material sense of self worth, which all the love in the world at home couldn't buy out in the real world.

They were different kinds of confidence—and as 50 explained, love from home and love for the game were as opposite as business and personal. As a rule, a young hustler knew better than to mix the two, but in his case, 50 was equally motivated by both, "(Air) Jordans come out, they cost $100…I don't want to ask her for the $100, you know what I mean, so I'm gonna try and figure out a way that I can get it. My mother, what she did before me, is what kind of showed me that that was a possibility. And it kind of felt like the only option."

Still, while 50 was perhaps drawn to hustling because it made him feel in some psychological way closer to his mother, hustlers were also drawn to 50 because his mother had been a hustler, perhaps suggesting an inevitability of sorts. In either case, the neighborhood hustling elders took 50 under their wing at the tender age of 12, having gone through what he was in earlier years, with his mother before she died, and perhaps they were therein equally as motivated to help 50, out of both a generic and more personal agenda, "I was uncomfortable asking my grandparents for certain things..."

"My grandparents had nine children, and they raised them at a time when shoes might cost $10...And times have changed: your shoes will cost you $125. Big difference. They raised their kids at a time when Pro-Keds cost $10. When I was a kid the new Jordans were more than $100...The people I met while I was with my mother, they had jewelry and nice cars...I wasn't comfortable asking (my Grandmother) to provide for me like that. So I asked the people who appeared to have it, who I had met through my mother's activities."

"People who had really nice cars and seemed to have the finances. They gave me an opportunity to hustle. So I started that early... Because I was Sabrina's little boy, (when I got older), they gave me three and a half grams—an eight ball. That's the truth. The same money I would've paid for those Jordans. Sometimes when you ask for fish, people give you a pole."

It also helped that 50 had the hustling heritage that he did, as it established an immediate street credibility for him in terms of trust, "Yeah, (my mom) did her thing...That's what made it easier to get involved with selling drugs, because all of the people that I had met when I was young were all people who sold drugs...The older dudes, they'd already seen me from when I was so big, so it was, 'Oh, that Sabrina's boy. He ain't gonna tell no one. He was raised doing this shit.'"

While 50 clearly feels his evolution into the life of a hustler, even at such a young age, was perhaps inevitable, he is quick to point out that it was, at first, his choice to do so, making a point to distinguish between the image of helplessness that often accompanies the reasoning behind why young African American males in the inner-city turn to hustling in the first place.

For 50, hustling became his only avenue once he had tasted its fruits and compared the immediately available alternatives, but he readily acknowledges that it was a conscious choice on his part to begin with, "I started when I was hustling when I was 12. Any 12 yr old kid that is not doing good in school and you tell him if you do good in school for 6 more years and you can get that car and then the kid's curiosity leads him through the hood to find someone who's got that car that didn't have to go to school that hustled…Well then it doesn't seem like one of the options, it seems like the 'only option.'"

The latter is important to 50 in countering any impression that something in his home life pushed him in that direction, and being extremely protective of his grandmother, the rapper goes to great lengths to illustrate the difference in the interest of avoiding assumption or labeling, "Gangsta is something that happened to me. That's not the way my grandmother raised me to be. That's the way the hood made me. You see a kid who isn't doing well in school and you tell him, 'Yo, if you do good for eight more years, you could have a car.' Then he finds out he can get a car in six months by running in the streets, and it feels like the way to go."

Still, 50 was expected to attend school regularly, and as his street education competed with his scholastic one, he struggled to find a balance that would allow him the opportunity to earn money without alerting his Grandparents to his activities, "I could hustle only after school. I told my grandparents I was in an after-school program…I was in a special program…The only time I could hustle was between three and six." 50 was fronted an 8 ball from the older hustlers both because they felt he could be trusted, but also because as a youngster, being busted with that kind of weight had less repercussion legally.

Likely, 50 was completely naive to that world of consequences entirely, focused instead on figuring out what to do with the opportunity that had landed in his lap. He got help from his fellow pre-teen dealers, explaining candidly that, at first, "I didn't know what to do with (the crack). Kids from my neighborhood helped me the first couple of times. Then I did it myself because I was eager."

Once he'd had a taste of the money, 50 explained that he caught on quick, "Once you get one person comfortable dealing with you, that turns into two, three, four people. As I got into junior high school I started hustling often… I used to leave my stuff at my friend's house and he'd leave his stuff at mine. At that point, we were only hustling for shoes and nice clothes."

At the tender age of 13, 50 was selling around his neighborhood to strangers, and family, without their even knowing he was the proprietor, such that, as the rapper explains, "My aunts and uncles would have a party, and like weed today, so many people used cocaine, it wasn't looked at like a drug. They would say, 'Go get some cocaine.' They didn't know I already had it."

Regardless of the naivety on the part of his extended family to the fact that 50 was a pusher-in-training, they did nothing to shelter him from the world of drugs in general, which could only have worked to make the whole lifestyle seem that much more normal to the young dealer, making his new profession that much more sensible. The gravity of the latter first hit home for 50 in junior high school, at the age of 13, when he was forced to shoot someone in defense of his life and livelihood, "(I was selling) Crack, a little heroine…"

"The first time I ever shot somebody, I was in junior high school. I was coming out of a project building—I ain't gonna tell you where. I was going to see this girl. I had my uncle's jewelry on, and two kids decided to rob me. This kid was like, 'Yo, c'mere, let me holler at you.' As I turned around they all started pouring out of the lobby. It had to be 15 people stepping to me to rob me. I had a little .380 six-shot pistol, and I didn't even look. I just spun around banging, 'Pop-pop-pop-pop-pop!' Shot and just kept running."

Once the reality set in on 50 in terms of what he had just faced, it didn't seem to deter him, rather just make him bolder. The situation also desensitized him, making him inherently more dangerous, a process 50 confirms and qualifies by explaining that "Yeah, I hit one of 'em. And that encouraged the next situation. After that, you get comfortable shooting. The first time, you're scared to death, as scared as the guy you're shooting at. Then it grows easier for you. Everybody has a conscience. You say to yourself, 'Man, he was gonna do something to me.' Then it's like, I don't give a shit, whatever."

"After a while the idea of shooting someone doesn't bother you." Following that experience, 50 became equally as bold in terms of his hustling, explaining that he became increasingly competitive in the course of describing some of the details of his drug operation, "I only called it 'buy one, get one free' because they were calling it 'two for $5' on the next block. I was trying to make it different. I was marketing!"

"Fiends want something free, so use the word free. It's better than 'two for $5.'…And (it worked, because) I made the pieces bigger. Some guys made small pieces and figured they would make a huge profit. But it takes them longer to sell the pieces. I made the pieces huge, and they started coming from down the block. All the pieces would sell the same day, and I'd accumulate more money."

As 50 accrued more capital, he also caught the attention of women, which taught him about the importance of looking the part as he was playing it, making him that much more competitive in the process, "Hell yeah. In the hood, your success is on wheels. It's about your appearance. When you first start, everybody is hustling for clothes, a different pair of sneakers every day so you're fresh all the time."

50 had been hustling for 3 years before the attention girls were paying him finally rewarded him with a home run, but he also explains his struggle around those bases taught him the importance of persistence, and remaining aggressive in all aspects of the hustler game, " (I lost my virginity when I was around) 15. I ain't shy. No means 'try again.' No, means she's in a relationship right now, but you try again when she's upset with him. A lot of pimps think like that too."

As a young teenager, 50 attended Andrew Jackson High School in Jamaica, Queens, and it was there that the young hustler was first exposed as a drug dealer to his strict, religious Grandmother after getting caught with drugs in school. 50 routinely hid vials of crack in his sneakers, and was caught in gym class one day after bringing the wrong pair of sneakers to wear.

As 50 explained the details of the arrest in more detail, "at that point I was hustling, so I used to hide (the crack) pieces from my grandmother. I had (the vials) in a pair of gym shoes, and I picked up the wrong shoes (to wear to school.) I went to school, and at the time at Andrew Jackson we had metal detectors. So when we went through the metal detection at the high school, (they ended up searching me and) they found the crack and they locked me up. I was out of school for a few weeks."

The incident also landed 50 on probation, and while the bust brought the spotlight onto 50, he didn't try to hide from the fact that his Grandmother had discovered what he was doing with his free time, explaining that, by that point, he was too deep into the game to get out, "after I got caught I had to tell my grandma…I was embarrassed that I got arrested like that. That's the worst way to get arrested."

"After I got arrested I stopped hiding it. I was telling my Grandmother openly 'I sell drugs.'…She asked me if the charges were true, and I don't lie to my grandma. As crazy as it sounds, I felt like I got caught because I was hiding it from her. I told her I did it, and I told her I was going to keep doing it. She was upset. She was hurt. She said, 'Don't call here when you get in trouble.'"

In 50's eyes, whatever wrong he was doing at the time was proportional to far worse, making it easier in his mind to justify what he was into given the comparative severity of what he saw others around him involved with, "Older dudes in our neighborhood were way worse. They were robbing banks; they would kidnap each other. They tried to rob me one night in front of my grandmother's house."

Aside from hustling, 50 also spent free time boxing during his early teenage years, which the rapper credits with helping to both toughen him up and give him patience, such that "after you box a little bit, you're conscious of your opponent's actions. And you're less emotional because you fight every day. So the fight doesn't mean as much. You're not fighting angry. You're fighting to win the fight, even in the street. I don't have to seem upset to react."

"If you say something and I feel like you should be punched in the face for it, my actions might not show you that I'm going to hit you. I'll punch you, and then we'll start fighting." Perhaps boxing also provided 50 an outlet for what he described later in life as a great deal of pent up anger over the life he was leading, "My most comfortable feeling is anger. If my feelings are hurt or if things don't go my way, I get angry."

For the most part as a teenager, 50 turned whatever his internal anger was into motivation, growing his game as a hustler exponentially, such that at the height of his teenage hustle years, at age

16, 50 dropped out of high school permanently, and became a full-time hustler, "(At my height, I was making) like $5,000 a day. I had a crack house on 160th Street with buckets of acid, so if the cops came, you would just push everything off the table into the bucket and there'd be no evidence."

50 viewed his growth as natural to the game's progression, wherein any hustler starts out small, and if he does what he's supposed to do, starts to become more entrepreneurially ambitious. To 50, it was a matter of basic logic, "a lot of times it takes money to make money...Once you acquire a little finance you can make some moves. Sometimes people do the wrong thing and enjoy it, some people provide for themselves by any means."

"If it comes down to 'I've got to go out and do something or the lights are going to go out', I'm going to do what I have to do to keep the lights on." Elaborating on what some of the more valuable lessons 50 took away from his experience as a drug dealer on how to be the best hustler you can be, the rapper reveals an impressive natural business acumen, in the process illustrating some of the parallels that street rappers draw between the earning potential for hustling and the rap game, "if you start hustling, then don't pay a person what they deserve, pay them what they accept."

"That's good business, even if you're not hustlin'. (You should still always) pay them what they accept, because you can capitalize off of people. In business, there's people who have talent and there's people whose talent is to take advantage of people who have talent. That's their talent, like Steve Stoutman—the guys behind the scenes get a lot of money."

To 50, and many like him, the mentality that is applied toward getting ahead in hip hop is no different from that applied on the streets, namely because the personalities in either situation are hardly ever dissimilar, and more times than not, one in the same, "(in either game), be prepared to do whatever you have to do. If you get put in a situation where your back is up against the wall, let your gun go off. You know, I mean I think if that doesn't happen, if that's missing from you that you'll be a victim. You know sometimes, either you are a victim or you victimize someone, and in the hood it's no holds barred—there's no way around that.

The kid in the schoolyard that doesn't want to fight always leaves with a black eye, you know what I mean? You can believe that, the situation come you gotta respond." Still, in spite of the latter, 50 has tried his best to maintain a business and personal distinction in the process, "You have to prepare yourself cuz everyone is not a bad person, when you walk in your home you don't have to maintain the same attitude that you had out in the street."

"You can be different with your people and your family than you are with a person that you run into in the hood, even them they have to know to respond to you differently in the hood cuz if people see something out of the character that they portray you…They'll try you… I have a problem with authority figures, I don't like people telling me what to do. If I respect the person's opinion, then I'm open. But if not, I ain't listening to nobody. Even with management, even my business, I have to respect the person to take their advice. If someone is like, 'You should do this because…just trust me,' they have to show me facts for me to understand what they're talking about or I ain't doing it."

"A lot of time for me to understand the music business, I have to internalize it in a negative way. I have to take it back to hustling in the street. Corporate America, when they can't give you more money, they give a title—you know, you feel better when you go to work as a manager at Burger King, but you still work at Burger King. Cause you ain't making burgers no more you're giving direction, you feel better. It's the same thing on the block: When the police comes so many times that half your crew is locked up and you have a few people left that know all the customers, you don't let them sell crack no more, you let them show the new kids how to sell crack, who to serve and who not to serve so they know that they're not serving the police. It's the same thing; I have to take it back there in order to fully understand it and see what's fully going on."

Almost a full decade before 50 ever achieved national popularity with rap fans, he had become a favorite of the local NYPD narcotics squad in his Queens neighborhood. As a result, he experienced his first real drug bust in June, 1994, at the tender age of 18, where, although a veteran of the crack game, 50 was about to make his debut as an 'on-record' criminal, becoming a convict within the New York Penal System…

"50 Cent—known as Curtis Jackson in indictments and record-ing contracts—was arrested twice in 1994 (the busts came three weeks apart) on felony drug charges. On June 29, Jackson and Taiesha Douse, his 16-year-old cohort, were nailed for selling four vials of cocaine to an undercover NYPD officer. According to court records— which you'll find on the first four of the following nine pages—Jackson steered the cop to Douse, who carried out the hand-to-hand transaction. When searched, Douse was found to be hiding 36 vials of crack in her panties and had 12 packets of heroin in a pants pocket, an NYPD evidence voucher shows. A lab analysis showed the pair's product to be 83.6 percent pure, so to speak. Jackson was nailed again on July 19, when cops—execut-ing a search warrant at his (Grandmother's) Queens home—dis-covered heroin and crack (rocks were hidden in a boot and a dresser drawer), drug packaging material, and a starter gun, which cops found sitting on top of a safe in Jackson's bedroom. Jackson pleaded out to both cases and was hit with a concurrent sentence of 3-9 years in prison…19 at the time, (Jackson) avoided hard time, instead spending seven months in a youth 'shock incar-ceration' boot camp in upstate Beaver Dams, (New York). (Jack-son's) parole term ended in January 2001…"

—Thesmokinggun.com

Chapter 3
June 29, 1994

When Curtis Jackson, a.k.a. 50, was arrested on June 29, 1994, he'd been a hustler for 6 years—3 part time, and 3 on a full-time basis. The latter was confirmed conclusively when 50 was again busted 3 weeks later, on July 19, pinched a second time for possession of crack cocaine, and heroine this time, with intent to distribute. Just as he hadn't with his grandmother, 50 made no attempt to avoid taking responsibility with the authorities for his drug dealing.

Instead, as 50 explained, he focused on how long he'd be out of the game based on the weight they had found him in possession of, "my lawyer said, 'I'll get you out in six months.' I said, 'What? Give it here.' I copped out right away, because they found a lot of shit in the house, and I thought the sentence would be a lot worse. I got arrested with 500 grams of cocaine."

True to his word, though 50 was handed down a concurrent 3 to 9 year prison sentence covering both busts, he was offered the option of serving his sentence at Brockton, New York's Lakeview 'Shock Incarceration' correctional facility, essentially a boot camp, where he spent 7 months inside. As 50 remembers the experience, "its' a boot camp, a lot of physical training starting at five in the morning."

"I had to accept a drill sergeant screaming in my face. You can not accept him screaming in your face and go do three to nine years in jail, or you can let them say what they gotta say and do six months. It's an easy decision. I was sentenced to three to nine years in jail. Because it was a nonviolent charge, I turned it into something a little easier."

Upon release from his incarceration, 50 was 20 years of age, and though he still went back to hustling, within the next couple years he would take a hard look at the path he was heading down as a hustler, especially now that he was an ex-convict on probation, and that getting busted dealing a third time would send him to prison for the full term of his original sentence.

The game had only gotten harder while 50 had been inside as well, such that he faced more of an inherent risk to his life when he went back to the streets, as the rapper explained in context of a robbery attempt shortly after his release from prison that became life-threatening, "I was 19 and had bought a 400 SE Mercedes Benz. I got to the front door, and the sliding door of a cargo van opened. They had a shotgun. I jumped over the porch and ran for a gun in the backyard. Pow! I got away from them."

"There's a strong possibility they would've killed me." For 50, his enlightenment to the idea that he might have other options came via two catalystic events in his life—the first being his introduction to legendary RUN DMC DJ Jam Master Jay, and the fact he had legitimate talent as an emcee, opening the door to the possibility of a future beyond the streets.

His second boost of motivation came in 1998, with the birth of his son, Marquise, "going to jail in those days wasn't much of a deal, because I had no one to take care of but myself. My little boy changed everything." Despite 50's apparent desire to get out of the hood via his pursuit of rapping, which eventually paid off, his grandparents continued to live there even after he'd made it to stardom, and moved his own family out, "(My grandparents are) really attached to where they live. That's what they have to show for their entire life."

For 50's part, following his meeting Jam Master Jay, he began to take rap seriously as a vehicle out of the ghetto, but never lost touch with his roots, a connection the rapper explains as necessary, even through present day, to keeping focused. In 50's estimation, by remembering where you come from and what you almost lost, an up and coming emcee can always keep perspective on both where he's at and where he's heading, "I work alot,…plus my hood (those two things keep me focused)…(In my hood), they love me on the music tip…"

"But not everybody is happy with me, there's always gonna be somebody who doesn't like you and there's some people that would like to kill me, (which keeps me down to earth.) It's got to, cause I can't move around like it's not there…I gotta be aware of what's going on, I can't afford to be lost…If I wasn't doing well I would still be in those situations. It's just like when you be in the hood you fightin over a corner, it's the same risk."

"When you doin well as an artist, someone may try you just to try you. When you respond, it's still on—so it's the same situation. It doesn't bother me, but I'm happy to be in the situation I'm in now. I feel blessed." Given 50's past, its not surprising he feels that way. Still, back when he met Jam Master Jay, long before Dr. Dre and Eminem, the emcee still had a long way to go…

CRIMINAL COURT OF THE CITY OF NEW YORK
PART AR1   COUNTY OF QUEENS

THE PEOPLE OF THE STATE OF NEW YORK
VS

1. CURTIS JACKSON
   DEFENDANT
2. TAIESHA DOUSE
   DEFENDANT

STATE OF NEW YORK
COUNTY OF QUEENS

POLICE OFFICER KATHLEEN KRAGEL OF QSNAG, SHIELD NUMBER 5846, BEING DULY SWORN, DEPOSES AND SAYS THAT ON OR ABOUT THE DATE OF JUNE 29, 1994 AT ABOUT 11:20 PM AT THE CORNER OF 134 AVENUE AND GUY R. BREWER, COUNTY OF QUEENS, STATE OF NEW YORK, THE DEFENDANTS COMMITTED THE OFFENSES OF:

PL 220.39-1   CRIMINAL SALE OF A CONTROLLED SUBSTANCE IN THE THIRD DEGREE

PL 220.16-1   CRIMINAL POSSESSION OF A CONTROLLED SUBSTANCE IN THE THIRD DEGREE

PL 220.16-1   CRIMINAL POSSESSION OF A CONTROLLED SUBSTANCE IN THE THIRD DEGREE

PL 220.03   CRIMINAL POSSESSION OF A CONTROLLED SUBSTANCE IN THE SEVENTH DEGREE

PL 220.03   CRIMINAL POSSESSION OF A CONTROLLED SUBSTANCE IN THE SEVENTH DEGREE

UNDER THE FOLLOWING CIRCUMSTANCES:

DEPONENT STATES BASED ON INFORMATION SUPPLIED BY UNDERCOVER POLICE OFFICER SHIELD #5428, THE DEFENDANTS EACH AIDING THE OTHER, KNOWINGLY AND UNLAWFULLY SOLD A NARCOTIC DRUG, TO WIT: COCAINE, TO A PERSON KNOWN TO THE DEPONENT AND THE QUEENS DISTRICT ATTORNEY
FURTHER DEPONENT STATES BASED ON DEPONENT'S OWN OBSERVATIONS THE DEFENDANTS EACH AIDING THE OTHER, KNOWINGLY AND UNLAWFULLY POSSESSED A CONTROLLED SUBSTANCE, TO WIT: COCAINE, A NARCOTIC DRUG, WITH INTENT TO SELL THE SAME.
AND THE DEFENDANTS EACH AIDING THE OTHER, KNOWINGLY AND UNLAWFULLY POSSESSED A CONTROLLED SUBSTANCE, TO WIT: HEROIN, A NARCOTIC DRUG, WITH INTENT TO SELL THE SAME.
AND THE DEFENDANTS EACH AIDING THE OTHER, KNOWINGLY AND UNLAWFULLY POSSESSED A CONTROLLED SUBSTANCE, TO WIT: COCAINE
AND THE DEFENDANTS EACH AIDING THE OTHER, KNOWINGLY AND UNLAWFULLY POSSESSED A CONTROLLED SUBSTANCE, TO WIT: HEROIN
IN THAT THE DEFENDANTS ACTED AS FOLLOWS:
DEPONENT STATES THAT ON THE ABOVE MENTIONED DATE, TIME AND PLACE OF OCCURRENCE SAID UNDERCOVER DID ASK DEFENDANT (CURTIS JACKSON) FOR A QUANTITY OF COCAINE. DEFENDANT (CURTIS JACKSON) DID THEN DIRECT SAID UNDERCOVER TO DEFENDANT (TAIESHA DOUSE). DEFENDANT (TAIESHA DOUSE) DID THEN HAND SAID UNDERCOVER A QUANTITY OF COCAINE (VOUCHER #F-529871) AND IN EXCHANGE SAID UNDERCOVER DID HAND DEFENDANT (TAIESHA DOUSE) A SUM OF UNITED STATES CURRENCY.

CONTINUED ON NEXT PAGE   PAGE NUMBER:1

CONTINUED FROM PREVIOUS PAGE

DEFENDANTS: CURTIS JACKSON, PLUS 1

DEPONENT FURTHER STATES THAT SHE, THE DEPONENT DID RECOVER A QUANTITY OF COCAINE TO WIT :(THIRTY SIX [36] VIALS CONTAINING A QUANTITY OF COCAINE, VOUCHER #F-529873) FROM THE UNDERPANTS DEFENDANT (TAIESHA DOUSE) WAS WEARING.
DEPONENT ALSO STATES THAT SHE, THE DEPONENT DID RECOVER A QUANTITY OF HEROIN TO WIT:(TWELVE [12] PACKETS CONTAINING A QUANTITY OF HEROIN, VOUCHER #F-529873) FROM THE POCKET OF THE PANTS DEFENDANT (TAIESHA DOUSE) WAS WEARING.
DEPONENT STATES AND STATES HE IS FURTHER INFORMED BY UNDERCOVER 5428 THAT THEIR CONCLUSION THAT THE SUBSTANCE PURCHASED AND RECOVERED IS COCAINE AND HEROIN IS BASED UPON THEIR EXPERIENCE AS POLICE OFFICERS AND TRAINING IN THE IDENTIFICATION AND PACKAGING OF CONTROLLED SUBSTANCES AND MARIJUANA.

FALSE STATEMENTS MADE HEREIN ARE PUNISHABLE AS A CLASS A MISDEMEANOR PURSUANT TO SECTION 210.45 OF THE PENAL LAW.

06/29/94   SIGNATURE

SWORN TO BEFORE ME ON THE
TWENTY NINETH DAY OF JUNE 1994

PAGE NUMBER: 2

comparisons, made by or at the request or direction of, the defendant, if the defendant intends to introduce such report or document at trial, or if defendant has filed a notice of intent to proffer psychiatric evidence and such report or document relates thereto, or if such report or document was made by a person other than defendant, whom defendant intends to call as a witness at trial; and (b) any photograph, drawing, tape, or other electronic recording which the defendant intends to introduce at trial.

MOTION TO SUPPRESS DEFENDANT'S STATEMENTS

The People respectfully urge that this Court deny the defense motion for the suppression of the defendant's statements or a Huntley hearing.

Upon information and belief, the source being, police reports, the People are unaware of any statements made by this defendant pursuant to Section 710.30 (1)(a) of the Criminal Procedure Law.

Accordingly, the defendant's motion for the suppression of the defendant's statements or a Huntley hearing should be denied in its entirety. The People are, however, prepared to go forward with proof of same should this Court grant a hearing.

MOTION TO SUPPRESS IDENTIFICATION TESTIMONY

The People respectfully urge that this Court deny the defense motion for the suppression of identification testimony or a Wade hearing.

The People submit that the undercover officer pointed out the defendant to the arresting officer shortly after the incident in question. Upon information and belief, the source being, police reports, the identification by the undercover officer occurred as follows:

➡ on June 29, 1994, at or about 11:20 am, in the vicinity of 134th Street and Guy R. Brewer Boulevard, Undercover Police Officer 5428 approached an apprehended other, Curtis Jackson, asking for a quantity of cocaine. The undercover police officer then walked with the apprehended other, where he directed the undercover police officer to the defendant, by pointing at her. When the undercover police officer approached the defendant, he showed her four fingers. The defendant then directed the undercover police officer to sit next to her on a bench, and subsequent thereto, the defendant handed the undercover police officer four gold topped vials of cocaine. Upon receipt of those vials, the undercover officer handed the defendant twenty dollars in pre-recorded buy money. The officer then left the location, radioing a field team the location of the defendant and the apprehended other, their descriptions, and an account of the transaction. Within minutes of the transmission, the arresting officer stopped the defendant and the apprehended other at the rear of 134-25 Guy R. Brewer Boulevard, who matched the description relayed by the undercover police officer. Within minutes of the above stated drug transaction, the undercover police officer identified the defendant and the apprehended other as the individuals who sold the four vials of cocaine to the officer.

As the Court of Appeals has made clear, where a viewing consists of a confirmatory identification by an undercover officer, as was true in the instant case, the defendant is not entitled to a Wade hearing. See People v. Wharton, 74 N.Y.2d 921 (1989). This principle is true as to stationhouse viewings, see, People v. Hill, 147 A.D.2d 500 (2d Dep't 1989)); on-the-scene viewings, see, People v. Allen, 162 A.D.2d 538 (2d Dep't 1990)); and as to photographic identification procedures, see, People v. Kearn, 118 A.D.2d 871 (2d Dep't 1986).

Accordingly, defense counsel's motion for suppression of identification testimony or a Wade hearing should be denied in its entirety. The People are, however, prepared to go forward with proof of same should this Court grant a hearing.

MOTION TO SUPPRESS PHYSICAL EVIDENCE

The People respectfully urge that this Court deny the defense motion for the suppression of physical evidence or a Mapp hearing.

Defendant has failed to state sworn allegations of fact constituting a legal basis for such a motion, as required by Section 710.60 of the Criminal Procedure Law.

Upon information and belief, the source being, police reports, the arresting officer, Police Officer Kathleen Kragel, Shield No. 5846, QSNAG was informed by Undercover Police Officer 5428, QSNAG that the defendant sold four vials of cocaine to Undercover Police Officer 5428 in exchange for United States currency. Undercover Police Officer 5428 radioed his back-up team and communicated a description of the defendant and the above transaction.

The arresting officer, Police Officer Kathleen Kragel, observed the defendant matching the description communicated by Undercover Police Officer 5428, and with probable cause, placed the defendant under arrest. Subsequent to a lawful arrest, Police Officer Kathleen Kragel conducted a search and recovered thirty-six vials of cocaine, twelve packets of heroin, one hundred and seventy-two dollars and twenty dollars in pre-recorded buy money, from the defendant's person. The arrest of the defendant was based upon probable cause, and the search subsequent thereto was lawful. Therefore, there were no violations of the defendant's constitutional rights.

Accordingly, the defendant's motion for the suppression of physical evidence or a Mapp hearing should be denied in its entirety. The People are, however, prepared to go forward with proof of same should this Court grant a hearing.

☑ ARREST EVIDENCE   ☐ DECEDENT'S PROPERTY   ☐ FOUND PROPERTY

☐ INVESTIGATORY   ☐ PEDDLER PROPERTY   ☐ OTHER

DATE PREPARED: 6-29 19 94   PCT. 113

Arresting/Assigned Officer		Rank	Shield No.	Tax Reg. No.	Command
KRAGEL, KATHLEEN		PO	5846	864487	QSRAG

Prisoner's Last Name	First	Age	Address (include City, State, Zip Code, Apt.)	No. of Prisoners	Acc./Aided #
DOUSE, TAIESHA S.		16	31-22 112 ST, CORONA, NY 11368	2	

Date of Arrest	Arrest No.	Charge/Offense Under Investigation	Fel. Misd. J.D. Vio.	Complaint No.
6-29-94	22783	220.39/220.16/220.03	☑ ☐ ☐ ☐	7669

Place of Property	Address (include City, State, Zip Code, Apt.)	Telephone No.
A/O KRAGEL, KATHLEEN	ONE POLICE PLAZA, NY, NY 10001	468-4864

Owner's Name (See Instructions)	Address (include City, State, Zip Code, Apt.)	Telephone No.
DOUSE, TAIESHA, S.	31-22 112 ST, CORONA, NY 11368	397-9339

Complainant's Name	Address (include City, State, Zip Code, Apt.)	Telephone No.
P.S.N.Y.	ONE POLICE PLAZA, NY, NY 10001	468-4864

ITEM NO.	QUANTITY	ARTICLE	CASH VALUE U.S. Currency only	DISPOSITION AND DATE
1	36	TAN XX TOP VIALS OF ALLEGED CRACK/COCAINE		NARC ENV# A467960
2	2	CLEAR PLASTIC BAGS		
3	12	WHITE PACKETS OF ALLEGED HEROIN		
XXXXXXXXXX	XXXXXXXXXXXXXXXXXXXXXXXXXXXXXXXXXXXXXXXXXXXXXXXXXXXXXXX			
	ABOVE IS A COMPLETE LIST OF PROPERTY VOUCHERED			
			TOTAL	

R.T.O.

REMARKS: Briefly explain why the property was taken into custody (see instructions on BACK OF BLUE COPY).

ABOVE LISTED PROPERTY VOUCHERED AS ARREST EVIDENCE. PROPERTY RECOVERED FROM DEFT'S UNDERPANTS (1-CLEAR PLASTIC BAG CONT 12 VIALS, 1-CLEAR PLASTIC BAG CONT 24 VIALS). 12 PACKETS HEROIN RECOVERED FROM DTHR F/K SMALL PANTS POCKET OF THE DEFT.

F 529873

POLICE LABORATORY

QUANTITATIVE ANALYSIS REPORT

LABORATORY NO. _94N054350P_ DATE _7.5.94_
item #1

A QUANTITATIVE ANALYSIS WAS PERFORMED BY THE
UNDERSIGNED. THE RESULTS OF THIS EXAMINATION
DISCLOSED _83.0_ % COCAINE PRESENT.

CERTIFICATION - I hereby certify that the foregoing
report is a true and full copy of the original report
made by me. False statements made herein are punishable
as a Class "A" misdemeanor pursuant to section 210.45
of the Penal Law.

Chemist Name _S. VAYSMAN_ Signature _____

Misc. 3758 (2-90)

Bruno

25

CRIMINAL COURT OF THE STATE OF NEW YORK
PART APAR COUNTY OF QUEENS

THE PEOPLE OF THE STATE OF NEW YORK v. CURTIS JACKSON DEFENDANT	STATE OF NEW YORK COUNTY OF QUEENS

POLICE OFFICER WALTER BURNES OF QSNAG, SHIELD 16822, TAX REG# 0889662, BEING DULY SWORN, DEPOSES AND SAYS THAT ON OR ABOUT JULY 19, 1994 AT ABOUT 8:50 AM ON THE SECOND FLOOR OF 145-40 ROCKAWAY BOULEVARD, COUNTY OF QUEENS, STATE OF NEW YORK,

THE DEFENDANT COMMITTED THE OFFENSES OF:
PL 220.21-1 CRIMINAL POSSESSION OF A CONTROLLED SUBSTANCE IN THE FIRST
          DEGREE
PL 220.16-1 CRIMINAL POSSESSION OF A CONTROLLED SUBSTANCE IN THE THIRD
          DEGREE
PL 220.50-1 CRIMINALLY USING DRUG PARAPHERNALIA IN THE SECOND DEGREE
PL 220.03 CRIMINAL POSSESSION OF A CONTROLLED SUBSTANCE IN THE SEVENTH
DEGREE

IN THAT THE DEFENDANT DID: KNOWINGLY AND UNLAWFULLY POSSESS ONE OR MORE PREPARATIONS, COMPOUNDS, MIXTURES OR SUBSTANCES OF AN AGGREGATE WEIGHT OF FOUR OUNCES OR MORE CONTAINING A NARCOTIC DRUG; KNOWINGLY AND UNLAWFULLY POSSESS A NARCOTIC DRUG WITH INTENT TO SELL IT; KNOWINGLY POSSESS OR SELL DILUENTS, DILUTANTS OR ADULTERANTS, INCLUDING BUT NOT LIMITED TO, THE FOLLOWING: QUININE HYDROCHLORIDE, MANNITOL, MANNITE, LACTOSE OR DEXTROSE, ADAPTED DILUTING NARCOTIC DRUGS OR STIMULANTS UNDER CIRCUMSTANCES EVINCING AN INTENT TO USE OR KNOWLEDGE THAT SOME PERSON INTENDED TO USE, THE SAME FOR PURPOSES OF UNLAWFULLY MIXING, COMPOUNDING, OR OTHERWISE PREPARING A NARCOTIC DRUG OR STIMULANT; KNOWINGLY AND UNLAWFULLY POSSESSED A CONTROLLED SUBSTANCE:

THE SOURCE OF DEPONENT'S INFORMATION AND THE GROUNDS FOR DEPONENT'S BELIEF ARE AS FOLLOWS:

DEPONENT STATES THAT AT THE ABOVE TIME, DATE AND PLACE OF OCCURENCE, HE EXECUTED SEARCH WARRANT #212 ISSUED BY THE HONORABLE BARRY KRON OF QUEENS CRIMINAL COURT. DEPONENT FURTHER STATES THAT HE OBSERVED THE DEFENDANT, CURTIS JACKSON EXITING THE BEDROOM DESCRIBED IN THE WARRANT. DEPONENT FURTHER STATES THAT THE DEFENDANT ADMITTED TO HIM THAT HE LIVED IN THE SAID BEDROOM.

DEPONENT FURTHER STATES THAT HE RECOVERED INSIDE THE SAID BEDROOM IN A BOOT BELONGING TO THE DEFENDANT, SEVEN PLASTIC BAGS EACH CONTAINING ROCKS OF CRACK COCAINE, EACH APPROXIMATELY ONE OUNCE IN WEIGHT. DEPONENT FURTHER STATES THAT HE RECOVERED INSIDE THE SAID ROOM, IN THE TOP DRAWER OF A

Defendant : JACKSON,CURTIS   Page 2

BUREAU THREE ADDITIONAL PLASTIC BAGS CONTAINING ROCKS OF CRACK COCAINE, EACH APPROXIMATELY ONE OUNCE IN WEIGHT. DEPONENT FURTHER STATES THAT HE RECOVERED IN THREE LARGE PLASTIC BAGS UNDERNEATH THE TELEVISION STAND IN THE SAID ROOM ASSORTED GLASS VIALS, VIAL TOPS AND RUBBER BANDS. DEPONENT FURTHER STATES THAT HE RECOVERED UNDERNEATH THE BED A GLASSENE ENVELOPE CONTAINING HEROIN. DEPONENT FURTHER STATES THAT HE RECOVERED AN AIR STARTER GUN ON TOP OF A SAFE LOCATED ON THE FLOOR OF THE ROOM AND SIX HUNDRED AND NINETY FIVE DOLLARS UNITED STATES CURRENCY ON THE FLOOR.

DEPONENT STATES THAT HE RECOVERED A TOTAL OF APPROXIMATELY TEN OUNCES OF CRACK COCAINE FROM THE BEDROOM AND HIS CONCLUSION THAT THE SUBSTANCE RECOVERED IS COCAINE IS BASED ON HIS EXPERIENCE AND TRAINING AS A POLICE OFFICER AND IN THE PACKAGING AND IDENTIFICATION OF CONTROLLED SUBSTANCES AND MARIHUANA.

> FALSE STATEMENTS MADE IN THIS DOCUMENT ARE PUNISHABLE AS A CLASS A MISDEMEANOR PURSUANT TO SECTION 210.45 OF THE PENAL LAW

DATE   SIGNATURE

SWORN TO BEFORE ME ON THE
DAY OF

SIGNATURE

SUPREME COURT OF THE STATE OF NEW YORK

PART __N 6 C__   COUNTY __QUEENS__   SCI , __QN 11741/94__
94Q024476

THE PEOPLE OF THE STATE OF NEW YORK

vs.

__CURTIS JACKSON__

DEFENDANT

WAIVER OF
RIGHT TO APPEAL

I, THE DEFENDANT HEREIN, HAVING BEEN CHARGED, IN AN ACCUSATORY INSTRUMENT FILED
AGAINST ME, WITH THE CRIMES OF ___220.21___ ___C.P.C.S. 1°___
AND HAVING BEEN INFORMED OF MY RIGHT TO A TRIAL OF THESE CHARGES, DO HEREBY WAIVE MY
RIGHT TO A TRIAL AND AGREE TO ACCEPT A PLEA BARGAIN DISPOSITION IN WHICH I WILL PLEAD
GUILTY TO ___220.16___

IN FULL SATISFACTION OF THE INDICTMENT AND BE SENTENCED TO ___3 - 9___

AS PART OF THE PLEA BARGAIN AGREEMENT, I HEREBY WAIVE ANY AND ALL RIGHTS TO APPEAL MY
CONVICTION

I WAIVE MY RIGHT TO APPEAL VOLUNTARILY AND KNOWINGLY AFTER BEING FULLY APPRISED OF MY
APPELLATE RIGHTS BY THE COURT AND MY ATTORNEY, _____, STANDING
BESIDES ME. I HAVE HAD A FULL OPPORTUNITY TO DISCUSS THESE MATTERS WITH MY ATTORNEY
AND ANY QUESTIONS I MAY HAVE HAD HAVE BEEN ANSWERED TO MY SATISFACTION.

__7/22/94__
DATED: / STATE OF NEW YORK

x _Curtis Jackson_
DEFENDANT

_____
ATTORNEY FOR THE DEFENDANT

THE ABOVE-NAMED DEFENDANT APPEARED BEFORE THIS COURT ON THIS DATE AND IN OPEN COURT,
IN THE PRESENCE OF THIS COURT, AND WITH THE APPROVAL OF THIS COURT AND WITH THE
CONSENT OF HIS ATTORNEY, SIGNED THE FOREGOING WAIVER OF HIS RIGHT TO APPEAL.

__7/22/94__
DATED: STATE OF NEW YORK

_____
JUDGE

"Jay's like King Midas, as I was told
everything that he touched, turned to gold"

—*Run DMC, 1986*

Chapter 4
Curtis '50 Cent' Jackson and Jason 'Jam Master Jay' Mizell

The true influence Jam Master Jay had on hip hop wasn't truly felt till after his tragic and senseless murder in 2002. While the legendary DJ was known as a third member of iconic hip hop group Run DMC, few knew that Jay's biggest accomplishment commercially since Run DMC's 1980s heyday was his discovery of a young unknown rapper named Curtis Jackson, a.k.a. 50 Cent, years before he blew up in 2002.

Jam Master Jay and 50 Cent both hailed from the same Jamaica neighborhood on the South Side of Queens, New York, and while 50 Cent was making his principle bread as a crack dealer in 1998, Jam Master Jay was also hustling, looking for up and coming talent to sign to his production company, toward the larger end of shopping 50 to major labels.

As 50 recalls, "A friend of mine introduced me to (Jay). It's funny—I was in the street, hustling, and I made some relation-ships, some people that I met...like, they knew people in the music business and they introduced me to Jam Master Jay. It's weird how who you know puts you on, and what you know determines how long you stay once you get there."

Perhaps the most humorous part of Jay and 50's chance meeting was the fact that Jay's 20 year old protégé-to-be didn't even know how to rap in an album context, as 50 explained, "(when) we met in '98, I could rap but I didn't know how to put it in song format and the melodies and cadences...Jam Master Jay is the first producer I ever recorded with, period. First record I ever record was with Jay in a studio in Rosedale. I didn't know how to write choruses, for example, and I learned that under him."

50 not only got his education as an emcee from Jay, at the time, he was rapping under plain old Curtis Jackson, and was encouraged by Jay to take on a professional persona, standard for any up and coming emcee in terms of establishing a street name.

Seeking to preserve his real life identity as a hustler as authentically as he could on tape, the rapper chose for his stage name one of Brooklyn's most notorious Crack lords, now deceased, "originally it was a gangster from Fort Greene Projects named 50 Cent and I took the name when he passed...He died, and every time they mention my name, that breathes life into him. It's not like Al Capone or John Gotti, or someone from the 'hood that wasn't active. He got killed, so I took on the name like that. It's actually from the 'hood, instead of from somebody that wouldn't even say 'what's up' to me if I seen them in real life."

Recalling in more elaborate detail the process Jay went through mentoring 50 Cent, 50 provides real insight into just how intricate the process of molding a raw street rapper into a professional emcee can be—in the studio—even before he ever thinks about stepping onto a stage or in front of a video monitor.

50 readily credits the DJ with teaching him all the basics about the basic recording of a song, "Well, he kind of groomed me, period.

Like, I had never been in a studio to record a record or make a demo or anything. That's the first time I was in a booth, in front of a mike, attempting to make a song, was with Jam Master Jay. Everything—my song structure, counting bars—I learned from Jay. That was the first time I ever went to the studio and attempted to make a record for real."

And while the fledgling star tried his best to remain focused as a student and avoid becoming starstruck, he admits in hindsight that it was difficult given the stature of his mentor. What 50 also reveals, perhaps for the first time about Jam Master Jay, was that, from a street perspective, Jay had the most credibility of any of the members of Run DMC, in part because he chose to continue working in the same neighborhood he'd come up in.

While this decision on Jay's part may have ultimately played a role in costing him his life, the keep-it-real edict of hip hop's truest street emcees was preserved immortally, seemingly important to 50, in hindsight and at the time, in terms of preserving the credibility of rap off the block, as it was moving more and more permanently into the mainstream during the later 1990s, "Jam Master Jay was a pioneer. We grew up watching Jay, so it felt crazy being around him. Like, when you were first around him, it was like, 'Yo, that's Jay!' You know what I mean? And he was like, the hardest member of Run-DMC."

As time went on, and 50 Cent became a more accomplished studio emcee, Jay began to seriously consider the possibility of signing his protégé to a major label recording deal, a dream come true for any inner-city hustler looking for a better life for himself, and many times for his family. In the case of 50 Cent, he had the latter motivation working for him by the time he and Jay were seriously discussing the prospect of landing 50 a major label recording contract.

50's son, Marquise, was born on in 1997, and having grown up without either of his parents, 50 wanted to both be around to raise his child, as well as ensure that he was financially and materially secure in ways the rapper had never been. As 50 recalls, "I knew I couldn't provide for (my son) and do the same things (I'd been doing, meaning hustling)."

The reality of being a father pushed 50 to become even more serious a student of Jay's, and to commit for the time to focus fully on becoming a successful recording artist, knowing at the time that Jay was his only shot out of the hustler's life, "I just went for it...In the music business, who you know will put you on, and what you know will determine how long you stay."

As fellow hip hop pioneer DMC recalls, during the latter part of 1998 and beginning of 1999, 50 Cent was constantly in the presence of Jam Master Jay, soaking up everything he could from the legendary DJ, both in and out of the studio, reflecting both an eagerness to grow as an artist, and a respect for the mentor who was guiding him on that path, "50 is an artist who actually hung with Jay when he wasn't in the studio...It was like, 'Yo, Jay taught me about bars, Jay taught me how to write hooks and what was the purpose. And Jay taught me how to write and make rap records. He made me want to really rap and do this.'"

Both Jay and 50 Cent's dream came true in 1999 when Jam Master Jay shopped 50 Cent through the DJ's own production company to several major labels, and ended up securing a deal for 50 with Columbia Records through the TrackMasters label, run by studio wizards Poke and Tone, at the time among the hottest producers in hip hop, having produced platinum singles for artists including Will Smith, Notorious B.I.G., LL Cool J, Blaque, Mariah Carey, Michael Jackson, Mary J. Blige, The Firm, Jennifer Lopez, and Foxy Brown, among others. The total value of 50's recording contract was for $250,000, with a $65,000 advance going to the rapper directly.

For 50 Cent, it was his first taste of success—on paper at least. Behind the scenes, things were more complicated than just a few signatures could or would explain, and the illusion that 50 was out of the hustling business forever quickly dissolved.

According to the terms of 50's deal with Columbia and Track Masters, he first had to be bought out from his contract with Jay's production company, to the tune of $50,000.00, which came directly out of 50's $65,000 advance, followed by legal fees, leaving 50 with very little money to live on, and forcing him to flip what he had left, and begin hustling again.

As 50 rationalized it, "Well, the deal at Columbia was for $250,000 and I got $65,000 in advance. I had a deal with JMJ (Jam Master Jay), so I negotiated for a release, and I gave Jay $50,000 and the attorney that negotiated the release with Jam Master Jay and negotiated the contract with (Columbia/ Trackmasters) got $10,000. (I was cool with Jay), because he took what he felt was his."

"I was never bitter at Jay, because what I learned from him is what allows me now to sell 10 million records. He groomed me. That's worth $50,000...(Still), I was left with $5,000. I bought crack cocaine with it—250 Grams. How else you gonna provide for yourself? I did thirty-six songs in eighteen days for Columbia. Then I had eight months go by with no work going on. I was selling crack through the whole album with Columbia because I had no option."

"How do you live off of $5,000 for over a year? You don't. And then (be expected) to move around like you're a rap star. How do you do that?" Still, in the grand scheme of things, 50 had his eye on the rap game as a way out, he just couldn't afford to wait around in the meanwhile given the responsibilities he had immediately before him, "The music thing was a positive move, and I felt like that's the way it was going... Everybody who sold drugs in my hood, the older people, are all in the music business now. If they're not in the business, they're protecting somebody in the business."

Aside from the slow movement on the release of his own album over the course of late 1998 and early 1999, 50 also felt at the time that he was being taken advantage of by Trackmasters in that they had him writing rhymes for other artists they were producing, ahead of releasing his own material, "I didn't want to just sit around and just [write songs for other people]. I would still go kick it with him and shit in the studio and make music. I think I recorded eight records and they were trying to give me two records."

"They wanted me to write music for Blaque. I wrote a couple of choruses for them, but then I fell back because I had to get my own shit together. Poke (had me) do…the chorus for LL Cool J's song 'Paradise'. (Once I got tired of it), I didn't even have a discussion with them…I just didn't deal with them anymore." Looking back on the situation now, 50 feels things have reconciled themselves to a satisfactory degree by the mere fact that he was finally paid for his work on other artists' records, reflecting the bottom-line focus of the hustler mentality, always at work in 50's case, "I've helped people make hit records… and even when you look at that [LL and] Amerie record, my name isn't there."

"We had a legal situation with that because they didn't put my name in the credits (but) they ended up paying…(Now) they've got to pay me." Once the focus finally came to center on 50, he was becoming desperate, hungry to get his shot at the brass ring, so he decided to take that shot in true gangsta fashion, with a pistol, jacking the brass ring itself, along with anything else he could grab along the way from the biggest rap superstars he was competing with at the time. Such that, in the summer of 1999, 50 Cent recorded and released his first commercial single, a brazen verbal assault on everyone from Jay-Z to Mariah Carey, aptly titled 'How to Rob'.

The song succeeded in garnering the attention of the industry alright, creating an arena-size ruckus among mega-egos that 50 had hoped it would. The song was designed to put the industry in check, reflecting the desperation of any young, inner city hustler trying to survive, let alone get out of the game. It reminded the industry that the bling-bling era was as vulnerable to lyrical jacking as was the elite status of its exemplars when something more authentic came along.

If nothing else, the song worked to keep hip hop's biggest stars on edge, which is exactly where 50 wanted them, listening and waiting for 50's next move. Hip hop had not heard a song like 'How to Rob' since Biggie Small's debut with 'Gimmie the Loot', and where Biggie's victims had been random, 50's were name-specific. While some industry-insiders, namely critics, questioned the wisdom of an up and coming rapper calling out his peers in such a bold fashion, without specific provocation, and in the process making them potential rivals, from 50's point of view, the song's logic made perfect sense from his street-corner vantage point, "When robbery's not out of the question, it's kinda easy for a song like that to fall into your thought pattern...Bigger artists have bigger diamonds.

Kids in the hood is looking at the TV, going, 'Damn it, look at that shit he got on!' Rappers have egos, so I was anticipating them being upset. But I didn't care, 'cause it had been a year since the deal with Columbia, and I'm still selling crack." In the end, the song's impact would back-fire in 50 Cent a short time later when, in May of 2000, he was shot 9 times in a now-legendary attempted murder that authorities and many industry insiders speculate was at least partially motivated by the song 50 had recorded and released almost a year earlier.

"Aiyyo the bottom line is I'ma crook with a deal
If my record don't sell I'ma rob and steal
You better recognize nigga I'm straight from the street
These industry niggaz startin to look like somethin to eat
I'll snatch Kim and tell Puff, 'You wanna see her again?'
Get your ass down to the nearest ATM...
When I apply pressure, son it ain't even funny
I'm about to stick Bobby for some of that Whitney money
Brian McKnight, I can get that nigga anytime
Have Keith sweatin starin down the barrel from my nine...
I'd follow Foxy in the drop for four blocks

Plottin to juice her for that rock Corrupt copped
What Jigga just sold like 4 mil? He got somethin to live for
Don't want no nigga puttin four thru that Bentley Coupe door
I'll man handle Mariah like 'Bitch get on the ground'
You ain't with Tommy no more who gonna protect you now?
I been schemin on Tone and Poke since they found me
Steve know not to wear that platinum shit around me
I'm a klepto nah for real son I'm sick
I'm bout to stick Slick Rick for all that old school shit
Right now I'm bent and when I get like this I don't think
About to make Stevie J take off that tight ass mink
I'll rob Pun without a gun snatch his piece then run
This nigga weigh 400 pounds, how he gon catch me son?...
Caught Juvenile for his Cash Money piece
Told him I want it all he said, 'Even my gold teeth?'"

—50 Cent, "How to Rob", 2000

Chapter 5
"How to Rob'

When 50 Cent came out with his first single, 'How to Rob', in the summer of 1999, he came out blazing! With fatalistic intentions, not to end his own life as a rap star, but rather as a hustler, he sought to challenge his competition in an old-fashion duel of words reminiscent of the small-town draw-downs between two Outlaws that settled beefs in the Old West. At the core of the song's strategy, 50 sought to present himself as a challenger, establishing himself as an immediate contender for hip-hop's crown, jacking it off the head of whomever was wearing it at the time, and robbing all its jewels in the process. 50 Cent was hip hop's no-holds-barred hustler, willing to do anything to make it to the top, stepping over whomever he had to along the way, wearing desperation on his sleeve, unapologetically doing what he felt he had to do to make up for Columbia Records dragging their heels on his release. 50 took rap back to the streets with his debut single, namely because that's where he still was operating from mentality wise at the time, "the thought process for 'How To Rob' is the thought process for the kids watching the videos in the hood. That's the type of robbery that makes sense; to rob a person for a half-million dollars worth of jewelry is a better situation when you know that when you rob somebody, your life is in danger afterwards. That is, if you don't wind up killing them in the process. You could rob somebody for $40 and they blow your head off because you just took their last $40. You could be in the midst of robbing ten people and one dude in that pack could only have $40 and he'll blow your head off for it. So, 'How To Rob' wasn't just me being creative, it was me going through, what I was going through. People misunderstand me for that."

As 50 elaborated in explaining why he, or anyone in his position of desperation, would, rather than watch in admiration, see a score when watching a bling-bling hip hop video, listeners got a rare glimpse inside the hustler thought process as it really occurs, specifically in terms of an analysis of motive, "When you're starvin…it's easy to come up with that concept, you know what I'm sayin? At that point, I wasn't doing well financially, so when you look at artists, bigger artists have bigger diamonds certain things that come with success. And you know the fact that they have money excessively allows them to buy jewelry excessively, buy cars and nice houses and everything else they want."

From a more commercial vantage point, which 50 also was capable of thinking of in the same time, he was seeking to make a big bang impression that could be comparable only to the sound and shock of a gun-shot, and looking back, the rapper has no regrets about the path he took to do so, "(I have no regrets), Nothing. 'I Rob' was the best thing I ever could think of (at the time), and I did it cuz when you're on a major label, there's a hundred artists on that label. You gotta separate yourself from that group and make yourself relevant. All I was doing with that record was makin everybody at one time say 'WHO'S 50 CENT? Who is this guy?' And it worked, it's effective to date."

"Every interview that I speak on they mention that and ask me about it—'How do you feel?' Well I don't care. When I made (that record), I was on a major label with Celine Dion, Mark Anthony, Mariah Carey, all of these big stars. I had to make a record that made people ask 'Who is 50 Cent?'" Being the opportunist 50 was with 'How to Rob' put him right on target with respect to the realities that any young artist, no matter how loud the hype around him is at the time of signing, faces from the corporate side once he becomes part of the bureaucracy that accompanies being a major label artist.

While he was without a doubt conscious of the latter as a result of his backburner status while signed to Trackmasters, 50 also seemed to instinctively know that the only way to battle his way through the red tape was to creatively outwit the stonewalling, to make himself not just noticed, but notorious in the same time, "Many people think that like when you sign a record deal as an artist, you made it. Naahh, its more like you got a opportunity to make it! Cause you don't have to be an artist. Most rappers feel like they artists in their owns rights, that's not the way you become an artist. There are things that come with being a successful artist (that you gotta do, above and beyond your own world)."

The process by which 50 conceived and recorded his breakout track reveals the genius of his creativity, specifically in his ability to spin talent and frustration into opportunity, in the midst of the pressure he was under—as a means toward some ends. Capturing the essence of his desperation on tape, the track was definitely hip hop lightning in a bottle.

And in the tradition of Ben Franklin, the starving emcee definitely had money on his mind, " I wrote 'How to Rob' in the car on the way to the studio, everything on it was kinda true. Everybody knew what I was saying, they just laughed at the fact that I would actually say it. The creative part was how I put it together." Not surprisingly, the fallout from the track was swift, immediate, and designed to damage 50 even as he made his play to shine, with his label receiving calls from the biggest names in the industry seeking an apology, or if nothing else, for the label to push a different single.

As 50 recalls, he wasn't giving out any apologies, because the root of the song—his desperation—was real, and after the song's release, there was no way he could retreat from his attack without permanently damaging his credibility. Besides, people were taking notice, "Yeah, they got phone calls at Columbia. They work differently right, I don't apologize for nuttin I'm doin. Its self explanatory, the record was. It didn't hurt anybody by saying this so if they take it personal fuck 'em! I looked at it like, you on a major label, it might be a hundred other acts, on that label."

"You gotta do something to separate you from everyone else that's there, to get you the focus for a minute. Like with 'How To Rob', people stopped and were like 'Who is that?', you know in the company itself (even.) After I released 'How To Rob', everybody knew who 50 Cent was, and were excited about 50 cent when he come to the building." The attention the song garnered at radio and within the industry also gave 50 the support of his label, temporarily at least, as executives saw dollar signs, and started pushing 50 to finish his album.

Among those platinum rappers who were now 50's overnight peers, he didn't receive as welcoming a reception, such that with certain stars whose egos were bruised or outright damaged by the song, he risked fan backlash because their following was more established. In 50's case, he still didn't give a fuck! He saw hip hop as the most competitive game on the street, and none of the artists he named off in the song were being called out personally, for 50, it was strictly business.

In his eyes, any reaction or slapback was just more spotlight for him, such that he welcomed it, and most importantly, anticipated and expected it, by the very design of the song in terms of strategy, "You know, I spoke about 30 people on 'How To Rob.'…Jay-Z was the largest person that responded to that record, and that's hip-hop. Hip-hop's competitive: It's almost like the new kid is reaching for something and you slap his hand away for doing it. It's all good, and I looked at it like he was offering me a title shot without making me go through the ranks. I appreciated it…I should send him some champagne."

The most important point 50 meant to convey through the song, after its initial impact, was that it wasn't personal with any of the rappers he called out in the course of the track, "(When) Jay-Z responded to 'How to Rob' when it first came out—that's hip-hop. (And eventually), he was able to get past that (because he knew it wasn't personal). If I've said anything in the past about someone that was really disrespectful, it's because I really don't like the artist. I wouldn't say anything (literally) unless someone is really trying to battle."

Less than a year after the song's release, as Columbia Records was readying the release of 50's debut album, the track would come back to haunt the rapper, on May 24, 2000, when he was shot multiple-times in an attempted murder that was definitely personal and serious to whomever ordered the hit. Arguably among the most valuable lessons 50 learned from the experience, aside from a reaffirmation in faith that God was watching over him (assuming one was even needed), was the fact that Columbia was definitely NOT Death Row Records, and that 50's kind of reality rap was too REAL for the taste of his corporate backers.

As such, the shooting came close to costing 50 not only his life, but also his chance at real success as an emcee, after Columbia Records shelved his debut LP, 'Power of the Dollar', and dropped him from their roster, "I didn't get a chance (then). Like, I was going to take off and then things happened, got interrupted. I dropped 'How To Rob', and the real single was 'Thug Love' with Destiny's Child—and then I got shot three days before the video."

"After that situation, your phone stops ringing. People are different. They're afraid of situations that they can't handle themselves. In the end, I found myself in a space where I had to market myself." In the aftermath, 50 had to start from nothing all over again—still, as he learned (literally) to walk again, he discovered, from a professional angle, that his reputation as one of New York's hottest underground emcees had been firmly planted, such that 50 immersed himself in the fledgling mixtape circuit, and slowly began rebuilding his life toward the goal of becoming a superstar.

His resilience is remarkable, but understandable from the street philosophy that 'what doesn't kill you only makes you stronger'. Looking back on his label's decision to abandon him at his weakest, after there release of the song 'How to Rob' had arguable assisted in facilitating the climate in which 50 was vulnerable to street-style retribution, the rapper is not bitter.

Rather, he prefers to point out the reality of major label hypocrisy when it comes to distributing gangsta rap music—namely in the fact that corporate executives love the money the genre produces, and will invest from that vantage point, but have no interest in understanding the roots of or reasoning behind the violence of that culture, or the importance to hip hop fans of authenticity within the music they're marketed—i.e., they'll always take the cash, but have no interest in knowing the source, "Columbia didn't understand 50 Cent; to them, people (like me) only get shot on TV. I was shot three days before I was supposed to shoot my first video ('Thug Love' with Destiny's Child). They freaked out. Major labels would prefer to work with 'studio gangstas', it's less of a risk."

"50 Cent was wounded in a shooting which took place on Wednesday morning in Queens, New York, while the rapper was sitting in a parked car with an acquaintance, 22-year-old Curtis Brown. The shooting took place on May 24 at 11:22 a.m. on 161st Street in the Jamaica section of Queens, according to a police spokesperson. 50 Cent, 24, was shot repeatedly in the legs and once in the jaw, while Brown sustained a hand wound...Brown was released and 50 Cent was admitted for surgery Wednesday morning, according to Jamaica Hospital spokesperson Michael Hink. As of Wednesday morning, 50 Cent was in stable condition. Because of a family request that no more information be given to the press, his current condition is unknown."

—*MTV.com News, May 25, 2000*

Chapter 6
9 Shots

On the night of May 24, 2000, while sitting in the backseat of a car in front of his Grandmother's house in Jamaica, Queens, 50 Cent was ambushed and shot 9 times with a 9 MM pistol. As 50 recalls his attempted murder, "I got shot out in front of my grandmother's house. It's like, it's right off the north conduit, South Jamaica. It's not a bad place for you to shoot somebody—you know, the parkway is right there, and so once you hit the corner and you turn and you're doing 70, you're not startling anybody, 'cause people are doing 70 up and down there all day..."

"It happened so fast that you don't even get a chance to shoot back...You can't move. Your first reaction is to move and then the shots are going off and you're jumping around the backseat. I was scared the whole time. Ain't nobody gonna tell you they ain't scared in that situation...(After they finished shooting) I was looking in the rearview mirror like, 'Oh shit, somebody shot me in the face!' It burns. Burns, burns, burns."

Looking back on his miraculous survival, 50 reasons that it wasn't his time yet, but that in theory, he could have had it coming because of his sorted past as a hustler, "I did some things that I'm not absolutely proud of. And I feel like it's karma. I think it's karma. I mean, I did some foul shit before, prior to me being shot. So it's kind of what goes around, comes around" 50's son was home with his Grandmother the night of the shooting, and heard the shots himself, despite the fact that he was at the time a toddler, "My son know. My son was in the house when I got shot. It happened in front of my Grandmother's house, and he heard the shots and then he see daddy in the hospital."

50's grandmother also heard the shots from inside her house and immediately called 911 for an ambulance. Fortunately, 50 was rushed to the hospital in time to save his bullet-riddled body from the death that should have befell him, for all practical purposes, and certainly based on the intent of the shooter. As 50 jokes now looking back, "(the guy shot me) all over the place—my pinky, the face, a lot of leg shots. The guy was a professional leg killer. He was a pro." Still, in reality, the rapper knows his survival was the only random element to the shooting, "it's a hit, man. You supposed to die in that situation. They're not playing."

In terms of how his Grandmother, who had raised 50 from the young age of 10, got through the attempted murder of her grandson, 50 explains that, in part, both were already desensitized to the reality of murders by the regularity of violence that plagued their neighborhood for years prior. On an emotional level, 50 explains that he got her past the incident by moving on with life himself, "(My grandmother's) all right. It's not unheard-of, being shot, where we from. It's like, if the only place you see that is on television, if you only see that on news, if you only hear about that or see it in a film, it might be traumatizing for it to happen and you just like, 'Yo, I can't believe this!'"

"But a lot of my homies ain't around. So it's like you go home and go, 'Mom, such and such got killed.' And you explaining it, to make her understand—it's not like blow it over, but it's easier for her to stomach it knowing how many other situations have gone down around us. Especially when you get back up and your fingers and your toes move, and everything good—you keep pushing ahead."

Upon arrival at the emergency room of Queens' Jamaica Hospital, doctors operated for several hours on the rapper removing bullets and bullet fragments from his riddled body, a process 50 experienced as one in which "the adrenaline is pumping so fast that the pain is not really that bad until the doctors finish with you. Then that morphine wears off and then you're introduced to the pain."

The process of recuperating from his injuries was a slow and painful one for 50, who was shot several times in the leg, in his right thumb (the shell of which exited through his pinky), his arm and in his mouth. The results of the injuries to his mouth included a bullet that lodged in his lower gum, shaving part of it off, knocking out several back teeth permanently, and leaving a bump in his tongue that is really a fragment doctors couldn't remove. In all, 50 spent 13 days in the hospital, and thereafter, 5 months in rehabilitation, during which he utilized a walker to move around, and endured a rigorous physical therapy routine and workout regimen that led to his eventual recovery.

Today, the only noticeable after-effect of 50's near-fatal shooting, aside from his physical scars, is a slight slur in his speech, which ironically added to his unique rap delivery style. In reflecting on the experience, 50 reaffirmed his faith in God, and belief that he had been put on the earth, and survived the shooting, for a sub-stantive reason, "I think anytime you're in a life threatening situa-tion and someone is standing a foot away from you...it makes you believe in God and (allows you to realize) you have a purpose and a reason for being because there are people who have things happen to them for no reason and they're gone."

"There are babies that are born dead and didn't have a chance to live. I got shot nine times and there's nothing wrong with my fin-gers and toes. Everything moves perfect. I don't wake up with my bones aching." One of the more seemingly bizarre aftereffects from the shooting for 50 personally, like many gunshot survivors, is that the rapper now finds he "can predict rain. Yeah, when it rains, I'm a weather center. I'm just as good as Channel 7 News." (Note: In 2003, the surgeon who tended to 50 Cent's wounds sued the rapper claiming that he hadn't been paid for his work.)

The irony of the civil suit lies in what it provides in the way of further detail into the immediate aftermath of the shooting. According to TheSmoking—Gun.com, "in a suit filed Monday in the Supreme Court of New York, an attorney for Dr. Nader Paksima alleges that the doctor treated Curtis Jackson for gunshot wounds and provided X-rays and post-surgical follow-up for months but hasn't received anything for his efforts. According to Dr. Nader Paksima, the 27-year-old rap star has stiffed him for more than $32,000 in medical bills...Paksima alleged that he operated on the performer at Queens' Jamaica Hospital and provided follow-up care."

In the days immediately following the shooting, even though 50 had survived the attempt on his life, his deal with Columbia flatlined. This concerned the rapper more than anything else because, as he explained, "it sounds crazy, (but) it hurt more to not know what I was gonna do with myself AFTER being shot. Like when I called Columbia Records and they didn't know what to do—like I was supposed to do a video with Beyonce and as soon as I got shot. They just like moved it. 'Well Beyonce's doin a record with Amil!' You see what I'm sayin, (they were stonewalling)."

"Then the Amil record came out, and I was in the hospital for 13 days, and I (kept calling) them up and they don't got no answers for me. There was no Plan B for me. If I don't make music, I'm going back to the hood. I'll sell crack. I'm gonna go back to sell crack if I can't make it in the music business, and that's because that's what I was doing before that. I never had working papers, I never had a job. I sold crack until I got in the music business. I make music cuz it's almost like I can escape everything I was involved in, alls I gotta do is make music. (I didn't know what I was going to do there at first.)"

Still, as 50's health improved, so too did the rapper's financial outlook, thanks to a publishing deal he signed while in the hospital based on the assumption that his album, 'Power of the Dollar', was still scheduled for release through Columbia. The publishing deal called for a $250,000 advance, half of which 50 was to receive upon signing, prior to the album's release, which he was in fact paid. As 50 explains the irony in events as they unfolded from that point, "I actually got shot and signed the deal in the hospital."

"I received the first half of the deal (advance)… 125K…I was supposed to get another 125K after the album was released, but right after I got it, Columbia found I got shot and dropped the deal… The company figured I got shot 9 times and I got in the face so they figured I couldn't perform, and used it as a tax write-off. So they drop me, but I owned my publishing again, and got a free $125,000… I knew I was gonna be alright, and I never needed for anything during that time period from the finances."

While the publishing advance cushioned 50's drop from the label, he wasted no time pretending that he was anything less than rap's next big thing, such that "the first thing I did when I got my paper was I went ahead and bought a Benz. I'm the kind of person that I feel I need things when I can't have them. Like, I felt like I needed a Benz, like I needed nice things."

From there, 50 began regrouping artistically, immersing himself in the New York underground mixtape scene, which allowed him to continue to build his street credibility, based on word-of-mouth about the attempt on his life, and the momentum he had started with 'How to Rob', coupled with his own rejuvenated hunger to make it, which was now stronger than ever, "as soon as I healed up I could've put the record out myself but I fell back and kept working the mixed tapes until I got the right deal."

From 50's vantage point, getting shot was a blessing in disguise as it related to his deal with Columbia Records because he got dropped, which the rapper viewed as a positive rather than as a negative as it allowed him to bring his music back to the streets, where his real fan base was, "When I was at Columbia, I would ask questions, find out what people's jobs were. If you put me in a hands-on situation, I'm gonna learn real fast."

"They didn't realize the importance of the black market and mixtapes, so I used the connections I made, and did what they weren't doing. And I had the worst deal, Ma, for like eight albums. If I didn't get shot, I wouldn't have gotten dropped from Columbia, and I wouldn't be in the situation I'm in now." The after-affects of the shooting on 50 personally seem to have been largely felt in a reaffirmed appreciation for the life God gave him and a renewed sense of purpose as it related to his career prospects.

Still, 50 appears to walk a fine line in revealing how thankful he actually is for the shooting in terms of the direction it took his career, explaining that among other downsides, "It hurts (to get shot). But it hurts more after the doc says you're going to be okay and the medications wear off. The healing process hurts more than the actual shooting. I got shot in the right hand, too. The knuckle on my pinkie is gone…I walk through a metal detector, and even though it doesn't go off, they still want to wand me. I got an aura around me that's negative, and I don't think it's gonna leave. But I'm all right with it. Everything happens for a reason.

Being shot in the face, I lost a tooth. Gums, too. And my voice changed. There's a little hiss when I speak, because there's more air in my mouth. And this is the voice that sells millions of records."

For his part, 50 has refused to speculate on who was responsible for his attempted murder, acknowledging only that his assailant is now deceased, and preferring to focus on the future in any discussion of his near-fatal past, "Kid dead...who shot me. He died three weeks later...I didn't know him when he shot me, but I found out who he was on the street...His street name was Hommo— that's short for 'homicide.' I don't know his real name...(In terms of why he came after me), it could've been a favor, or he could've been paid."

"The kid who shot me was a rider—he came to kill me. You understand? He wasn't bullshitting. It just wasn't my time to go... Anyone you call professional would've gotten the job done... He got killed two weeks later. I'm uncomfortable answering these questions because people will think I might've done it. That's the kind of shit that could fuck me up. Everything is going so good for me right now. I just want to move forward."

The NYPD continues to classify the case as an 'unsolved attempted homicide', one government agency who has established a theory into which parties are responsible for ordering the shooting is none other than the Internal Revenue Service. According to an IRS affidavit filed in connection with a wide-sweeping investigation into 50 Cent's nemesis, Murder Inc., and the label's connections to drug lord Kenneth 'Supreme' McGriff, it was McGriff who ordered 50's murder, in addition to McGriff's financing the label with drug profits, and subsequently using the company to further his criminal activities and launder additional illegal proceeds derived from McGriff's various nefarious enterprises.

As summarized by TheSmokingGun.com, who uncovered the affidavit prepared by IRS Agent Francis Mace, "Murder, Inc., rap music's hottest record label, is secretly controlled by a notorious drug kingpin who engineered the shooting of 50 Cent, music's newest superstar, according to a recently unsealed government filing.

The label, run by Irv Gotti (real name: Irving Lorenzo), was allegedly bankrolled by his childhood friend, Kenneth McGriff, the convicted head of the 'Supreme Team,' a murderous drug gang that once terrorized Queens neighborhoods, according to a 32-page affidavit sworn by Internal Revenue Service agent Francis Mace. The IRS affidavit was filed in January in support of a successful government attempt to seize bank accounts related to 'Crime Partners,' a movie produced by McGriff and some cohorts from Murder, Inc., which bills itself as 'the world's most dangerous record company.'

The straight-to-video release stars Ja Rule, Murder, Inc.'s top recording artist, and other rap luminaries like Snoop Dogg and Ice-T. The IRS affidavit portrays McGriff as the power behind Murder, Inc., quoting a confidential informant as saying that 'while Gotti is the public face' of the label, McGriff 'is the true owner of the company. It is well know in the music industry that McGriff has provided Murder, Inc. with 'muscle'—threats, violence, and intimidation.'

Agent Mace describes McGriff as a weekly visitor to Murder, Inc.'s Manhattan office, where the convicted felon 'knows where the CEO's keys are hidden' and has been involved 'in the negotiation and review of business contracts on behalf' of the label, a division of the Universal Music Group. McGriff also allegedly laundered money through Murder, Inc., which covered a variety of the convicted felon's expenses and also gave him 'large sums of money' (McGriff was never paid in his own name, but through several 'false identities'). In a two-way pager message quoted by Mace, McGriff—who is now in prison awaiting sentence on a parole violation—bragged that his reputation keeps people 'in line' and serves as a warning to others to 'never fuck with' the rap label."

According to the specific language within the affidavit addressing the allegation that McGriff was responsible for facilitating the attempt on 50's life, Agent Mace alleges, on page 15 of the 32 page affidavit, that "the investigation has shown McGriff's involvement in homicides and a shooting. These acts of violence have been linked to both narcotics trafficking and the rap music industry. In one instance, McGriff directed co-conspirators to kill a drug associate who, agents believe, McGriff suspected of cooperating with the government. In another instance,

McGriff was involved in the shooting of another rap artist named '50 Cent' who wrote a song exposing McGriff's criminal activities. Confirmation of McGriff's violent activities are demonstrated by reliable, confidential informants; toll analysis of the Murder, Inc. pager; and evidence obtained via search warrants at a narcotics stash house where McGriff's fingerprints were recovered." McGriff is currently serving a 3 year prison sentence for a parole violation related to his possession of an illegal and unregistered handgun, and the government investigation into McGriff and Murder Inc. continues through present day.

The connection between McGriff and Murder Inc., Irv Gotti and Ja Rule as it relates to 50 Cent's shooting and subsequent beef with Irv and Ja Rule is hardly coincidental, and warrants further investigation. In the aftermath of the shooting, 50 Cent reflected a resignation to the fact that fate is largely out of his hands, beyond his belief that he was spared for a reason, be it his career or something greater.

The latter point he is still pondering, "I accept that death is going to come. So I don't fear none of these niggas. Death is a part of the largest form of entertainment. Action films are all based on scenarios that, if we were doing them, we could possibly die. It's hard to wake up ambitious tomorrow if you spend today thinking about dying...I feel like it changes your life a lil bit. Like when you get shot at nine times (and survive), you start makin a dream for a reason. You got a purpose. I'm still tryin to figure out what my purpose is."

In the interim, 50 has taken heavy precautions to ensure that he is much better prepared for any future attempts on his life. While some might argue that this is paranoid, 50 would readily agree, and justify the paranoia as logical considering the randomness of death's timing, "That paranoia stays with you: that it's possible that it will happen again. That is why I take precautions. I travel in a bulletproof car and I wear a bulletproof vest, always."

Still, while 50 traveled with heavy armory after the shooting, he still traveled, moving forward in his quest for greatness, believing more than ever that his survival meant he had a larger purpose, a message to deliver from God, and that perhaps hip hop was his instrument with which to do so. More than anything, 50 seemed determined not to cast his life in the role of victim, focusing on the positive, and pointing out that, ultimately, "death is promised to all of us. Where did Pac get killed? That passenger seat. Where did Biggie get killed? That passenger seat. Where did 50 Cent get shot? The backseat, but still in the car, shooters are comfortable shooting in vehicles so I've got a bulletproof vehicle."

"I'm a target, but I don't dwell on it…I got shot blocks away from where Jay was killed. I get excited about things I can prevent…I have to stay focused and keep working…I think I'm supposed to do something positive, more positive. The fact that I exist is saying there's always a possibility. There's always hope. As far as getting shot, they say time heals all wounds. And when I talk about getting shot, it doesn't hurt all over again. Your memories of pain are a lot less than when you're going through pain. So it's not a big deal to me. I got shot nine times. The big deal is you start thinking that he shot you nine times and didn't finish you—that makes you feel like you have a purpose, a reason for being…"

"Besides the fool being a professional leg shooter, you gotta feel God made the shells land where they land, so I look at all my situations and everything that I go through…(and) I'm still trying to figure out what my purpose is; I think it's something positive."

SUPREME COURT OF THE STATE OF NEW YORK
COUNTY OF NEW YORK
--X

NADER PAKSIMA,   :

    Plaintiff   : **VERIFIED COMPLAINT**

  -against -   :

CURTIS JACKSON, a/k/a CHARLES   :
JOHNSON, a/k/a, "50 CENT",

    Defendant.   :
--X *03108192*

  Plaintiff, NADER PAKSIMA, by his attorneys, MYERS & GALIARDO, LLP, as

for his Verified Complaint herein, respectfully sets forth the following:

1. At all times hereinafter mentioned, plaintiff NADER PAKSIMA was and

is a resident of the City, County and State of New York.

2. At all times hereinafter mentioned, defendant CURTIS JACKSON, a/k/a

CHARLES JOHNSON, a/k/a, "50 CENT" [hereinafter referred to as "CURTIS

JACKSON"] was and is a resident of the City and State of New York.

3. At all times hereinafter mentioned, plaintiff NADER PAKSIMA was and

is a physician duly licensed to practice medicine in the State of New York.

4. At all times hereinafter mentioned, plaintiff NADER PAKSIMA was and

is a physician working at Jamaica Hospital Medical Center, located in the County of

Queens, City and State of New York.

5. On May 24, 2000, defendant CURTIS JACKSON presented to Jamaica

Hospital Medical Center with multiple gunshot wounds.

6.   On May 24, 2000, plaintiff NADER PAKSIMA treated defendant CURTIS JACKSON for the aforementioned gunshot wounds, including the use of surgical intervention.

7.   On June 14, 2000, plaintiff NADER PAKSIMA treated defendant CURTIS JACKSON for the aforementioned gunshot wounds, including the use of x-rays and post-surgical follow up treatment.

8.   Subsequent to June 14, 2000, plaintiff NADER PAKSIMA treated defendant CURTIS JACKSON for the aforementioned gunshot wounds with follow up treatment related to the surgical procedures.

9.   Defendant CURTIS JACKSON agreed to pay and is obligated to pay for the medical treatment he received from plaintiff NADER PAKSIMA.

10.   The bill for the medical services and surgery provided by plaintiff to the defendant are in the amount of $32,511.87.

11.   Despite repeated requests for payment to date, the sum of $32,511.87 and continuing remains due and owing to plaintiff.

12.   Consequently, plaintiff has to date sustained damage in the sum of $32,511.87 and continuing.

WHEREFORE, the plaintiff NADER PAKSIMA demands judgment against the defendant CURTIS JACKSON, a/k/a CHARLES JOHNSON, a/k/a, "50 CENT" as follows: in the sum of $32,511.87, together with interest, costs including attorneys fees and disbursements in this action.

DATED: New York, New York
April 30, 2003

YOURS, etc.

Christopher D. Galiardo

MYERS & GALIARDO, LLP
122 E. 42nd Street, Suite 2710
New York, New York 10168
(212) 986-5900

VERIFICATION

STATE OF NEW YORK)
)ss.:
COUNTY OF NEW YORK)

NADER PAKSIMA, being duly sworn, deposes and says that deponent has read the foregoing SUMMONS and VERIFIED COMPLAINT and knows its contents; the same is true to the deponent's knowledge, except as to those matters stated to be alleged upon information and belief, as to those matters, deponent believes them to be true.

NADER PAKSIMA

Sworn to before this
30th Day of April, 2003

Christopher D. Galiardo
Notary Public, State of New York
No. 02GA6048827
Commission Expires October 2, 2006

Photos

Part 2
Introduction

As 50 continued his rule of hip hop, both as a label head and artist in his own right, part of his victory came through persevering past beefs that had threatened to bring him down in the beginning of his career. His strategy for success, aside from a relentless work ethic, had been simply to keep-it-real, even as the money began rolling in.

While this paid off handsomely for 50, things had not panned out so well for arguably his biggest rival, Murder Inc., whose flagship artist, 50 nemesis Ja Rule's, last two albums, 2003's Blood in My Eye, and 2004's R.U.L.E., had both flopped commercially, failing to sell more than a million copies collectively.

More seriously however, on a personal level, on January 26th, 2005, label C.E.O. Irv Gotti, along with his brother Chris, were arrested by the F.B.I. and charged with money laundering. According to *USA Today*, "the hip-hop label behind music superstars Ashanti and Ja Rule was part of a murderous criminal enterprise that protected its interstate crack and heroin operation with calculated street assassinations, federal authorities charged Wednesday... Label head Irv "Gotti" Lorenzo and his brother Christopher surrendered to the FBI on money-laundering charges Wednesday as federal prosecutors unsealed an indictment seeking to confiscate all the assets of their label, "The Inc"...their childhood friend, Kenneth "Supreme" McGriff, one of New York's most notorious drug kingpins, was charged with murder, racketeering and other crimes that prosecutors said were intended to eliminate and intimidate potential witnesses…He already was in prison on a relatively minor gun charge…Prosecutors believe McGriff and the Lorenzos funneled hundreds of thousands of dollars in drug profits through The Inc., a chart-topping label owned partly by Island Def Jam, a Universal Music label…Federal agents began to close in on McGriff and the Lorenzos in recent months with arrests that netted Ja Rule's manager and a bookkeeper for The Inc. At least five other defendants, including associates of McGriff, already have been charged."

"…McGriff, 44, was founder of the Supreme Team, once one of the city's most violent drug crews. Investigators suspect that after he finished serving about nine years for drug conspiracy in 1997, he set about reviving his lucrative—and deadly—drug-dealing operation…Cooperating witnesses have told investigators that McGriff admitted to the 2001 revenge slaying of up-and-coming rapper E-Money Bags. Prosecutors also believe he arranged the Baltimore killing one month later of a suspected informant in his drug organization. Another man also died in the Baltimore shooting."

MTV.com news, in elaborating on the indictment, reported that "after the hearing, Irv Gotti made a brief statement. 'I'm gonna give you guys one comment. I want to make it very crystal clear that I don't look (badly) at the government in any way, shape or form for them thinking I'm doing anything wrong. I call myself Gotti, I made my label Murder Inc., I grew up poor, from the street. But I don't look bad at them for thinking ill things of me. In no way have I done anything wrong except make great music that people seem to love. That's all I'm guilty of.'…"

New York City Police Commissioner Raymond Kelly said at a press conference Wednesday afternoon that 'They don't call it gangsta rap for nothing — the thug image isn't accidental…This is not an indictment of rap music. If you're involved with money laundering or drug dealing or committing murder, we're coming after you, irrespective of (the music). That's our business.'...The assets of McGriff's companies, Picture Perfect Films and Picture Perfect Enterprises, have been seized; their combined worth is approximately $425,000. Authorities are seeking to seize the assets of the Inc. and the affiliated IG Records as well..."

McGriff, along with eight associates, has been indicted for racketeering, illegal use of firearms, drug distribution and homicide. The associates include Inc. bookkeeper Cynthia Brent, who was arrested on money-laundering charges in November and released on a $200,000 bond; Ja Rule's manager, Ron 'Gutta' Robinson; Vash-Ti Paylor; Nicole Brown; Dennis 'Divine' Crosby; and Victor Wright." For 50's part, his final commentary on the Gotti beef was one in which "I think it's sad (about) Irv Gotti's situation. He's the guy who allowed his blessings to turn into something negative. After establishing himself in the music business, he tried to become something he never had the heart to be in his neighborhood. That's where "Gotti' came from. He was DJ Irv ahead of that. Anybody that's in the street is trying to get out. You can't blame anyone but Irv." 50, surprisingly, had less harsh words for Ja Rule, sympathetically stating that "I might sign Ja Rule when he's done at Murder Inc. After I destroy him, I'll rebuild him."

Beginning in early 2004, 50 Cent began work on his highly anticipated follow-up to Get Rich and Die Tryin. Slated for a mid-February release, the album was initially entitled 'The St. Valentines Day Massacre', although, according to 50, the only battle he was having on street date was "competing with myself... Anything less than 11 million records would be a failure, I'm talking about the end of the record. With the first album I felt like I failed because anything I was doing, I was doing for the first time. I know what I'm doing this time, last time I was like 'ok, what am I supposed to do?' and I didn't really know...If there were something else going on that would excite me. I have to use Em as my balance. In his career he continues to go uphill. And I feel like that's what's happening to me. I surround myself with the kind of people that I can accept criticism from. Everyone has an opinion. But I don't accept everyone's opinion. I know Em and Dre are in my best interest. I respect them and I listen to them. In so many ways Em gets me excited about things that no one else can get me excited about. I was on my DVD for The New Breed before I came out with Get Rich or Die Tryin' and they asked me what do I fear. I said I fear not fitting in with Eminem and Dr. Dre."

"All of these other issues in the street and you fear not fitting in? I said, yes because all of those things are the norm from where I come from and this is the new exciting thing for me to be able to fit in with them. I've been progressing at a pace that I think is cool but I can progress at an even faster pace. They should look forward to me releasing even more material that has the same quality over a shorter time span than last time. I had to wait. I set Banks and Buck up with Beg For Mercy and then they released their solo projects. I don't have to wait any more."

In fact, 50 would have to wait, just a bit longer, while his next G-Unit superstar—The GAME—blew up in the same big-bang that 50 had come out of the gate with, in a move 50 explained as one in which "I had to move it back because of my Game record...(I'm) not disappointed because I'll still be able to use a lot of things I had planned for it but I really did want a release on February 15th..."

"I was trying to force Interscope Records to release my record on February 15, but Interscope Records is reactive. I'm proactive, so I threw 'Disco Inferno' out and kinda got them to respond to me. But (The Massacre) probably wouldn't even be coming out March 8 if I didn't do that at that point, because this project is a big project to them, they want to have everything mapped out and it's more mechanical this time."

When he wasn't in the studio, 50 followed his mentors Eminem and Dr. Dre into the boardroom, launching G-Unit Records into an active label, releasing albums by Lloyd Banks, Young Buck, and in early 2005, The Game. The latter emcee, hailing from Compton, California, was brought into 50's fold at the suggestion of Interscope chief Jimmy Iovine, much in the way he had first brought Eminem to the attention of Dr. Dre years before.

While the Game was signed officially to G-Unit through Aftermath, and was motivated for his own part, as a Compton native, by the opportunity to work with Dr. Dre. The teaming with 50 Cent in a mentoring relationship followed the tried-and-true formula that had worked first for Dr. Dre and Eminem, and then for Eminem and 50 Cent, and secured the Game instant credibility with the record buying public on a national level.

As 50 Cent reasoned, "I think it's interesting to see how (the public will) embrace the (Game's) record since he's coming from the West Coast…What I been trying to do is diversify the perception and the vibe of G-Unit. This is another artist who speaks about another environment, being from Los Angeles, but he's aggressive also."

In terms of 50's relationship personally with the Game in contrast to fellow G-Unit crew mates Lloyd Banks, Young Buck, and Tony Yayo, 50 explained that "we have a different relationship, I've known Lloyd Banks and Tony Yayo all my life, Young Buck isn't so closely into the camp, he's spent the last 2 years around me. So it will take time for me and Game to develop the same relationship that me and the rest of the crew have but he's a part of the crew like everybody else and I want to add it to you that his first week sales just came and he sold 586,933 records…Game's first week, it's exciting for me to have an artist come out and go gold the first week, especially when Ja Rule's record is out there and he's at 538,000 records right now. Game's sold more than Ja Rule in his first week after his album's been on sale for 10 weeks."

For the Game's part, he explained that "I opted for Aftermath since Dre was from Compton, I'm from Compton, you know… I'll keep the whole N.W.A legacy going….That's where I wanted to be…Dr. Dre, he got his own way, his order of operations that he likes to have…And he had the successes of Snoop Dogg, then Eminem, then 50 Cent, then myself coming up, batting cleanup. He got the magic, man. At the end of the day, I wouldn't be nothing without Dre's beats. Without Dre's (and 50's) tutelage and (them) mentoring me for the last two-and-a-half years we wouldn't be standing out here doing this interview and I'd probably be part of the crowd and somebody else would be talking to you."

With the Game's release safely in the bag, 50 Cent throughout the month of January and the early part of February, continued last minute touch-ups on what he hoped would be his masterpiece, such that "The Massacre, I think it's better than Get Rich or Die Tryin', honestly…I spent a lot of time, put a lot of details into it. I actually took longer recording this record than I did Get Rich or Die Tryin'…When I started, I went in and did like 14, 15 records…Then I put those records aside and started over. I went out to L.A. and worked with Dre. We got some special joints so I'm excited right now. I know I'm gonna exceed everyone's expectations on this project because they feel like Get Rich or Die Tryin' was the best I could do. I got something up my sleeve."

Elaborating on their collaboration in the studio, Dr. Dre explained that, the second time out, "it is pretty much the same technique—we go in, I have some tracks ready and he just comes in and does his thing…I think the last time we worked (it took) what, about a week?…We just worked about a week on the record and I think we put in about two weeks this time…You know what's going to happen—it is going to be crazy."

50's confidence in his sophomore effort secure based on the inclusion of Dre's sure-platinum-fire beats, the rapper boasted that "I guarantee this album will be 10 times better than my first record. It's a little more complex. Now that I know people are listening, I can articulate and write the things I wanna write. My first record, I was just trying to have fun with it and express my actual situations. I write about the harsh realities. I'm just interested in seeing how they respond to it."

Elaborating on the making of his new album, 50 explained that "it's a continuation from Get Rich or Die Trying; I took a photograph and added illustrations to it. It got a flip-off cover and then there's a whole other artwork. It's exciting cause what I did for my album insert is I picked photographs to go inside with the lyrical content of some of the songs to give you a visual of what I'm saying."

"You know, I listen to the music when I buy a CD and I stare at the pictures so what I do is I make the pictures actually feel like they're tied to the songs...There's (also) some major differences between these records. I went back, I put the things that I missed on Get Rich or Die Trying and I added a lot of details. I feel like this record is better than Get Rich or Die Trying. I can't wait to see how the general public embraces it...(The producers on the record include) Eminem, Dr Dre, Scott Storch, Hi-Tek, Needlz, Buckwild, 4 or 5 new producers cause when I listen to the beats, I have (people) take off the names of where the music came from, so when I listen to it, I'm just listening to it for the music, not for who made it..."

"When they send me music, I have them send it to me with no label on it. All I'm listening to is music. I'm listening to it with fresh ears. I'm not being altered because Neptunes made it. Sometimes that changes your perception of the record. You'll want it to be good. Because of who made it...Even on this project you'll see a lot of new guys, various production. On Beg For Mercy it was like that too. At the end we recorded four songs with Dre. We had one day in LA...We took full advantage of it. All four of the records went on the album...I recorded 11 records in 3 days, I really did! And then I kept 4 of 'em cause I felt they were a good representation of me, from Get Rich Or Die Trying till now. But the records are great so in the future you'll probably hear some of those records..."

"One of my favorite songs is 'A Baltimore Love Thing'…It's titled that because in Baltimore the heroin addiction rate is really high. So the song is about the relationship between an addict and the drug. I give this drug a motion, feelings and at some point in the song, the drug actually becomes mad at the addict for trying to leave. It's like a real vivid description of what it would be like if it was human…You hear people make references to drugs-talking and people who are addicted to it. So what I did is I created a song where I'm actually the drug talking to the person…"

'I don't have an A&R department when it comes to my project," he explained. "I get so personal with it that I've got to kind of pick everything myself. So I have them take the music that's sent to us and have them put it onto a blank CD and just put a number on the CD instead of just sending me the name of the actual producer. Sometimes you lean toward music that is produced by a great producer, someone that you have respect for, and you may pick something that ain't actually the hottest thing."

50's first single for the new album, 'Disco Inferno', was released in late December, 2004, and by mid-January, 2005, had cracked the top 5 on Billboard's Top 200 Singles Chart. 50, for his part, was visibly excited about the public response to his first single off the new album, as well as the second single, 'Candy Shop', remarking that "the record's done incredible… It's #4 in the country right now, and it had zero support from Interscope Records."

"I went out with it with or without them and they caught up to it. They ended up sending (out official promos) after I MP3ed it across the country. I feel good about it, and now I'm ready to move into The Candy Shop…It's a little…it's edgy…I think the song itself is great…I attempted to be as sexual as possible, from a male perspective, without being vulgar or obscene. I think that I did a great job on it."

"The video itself, visually, me and (director) Jessy Terrero came up with the treatment for. It's exciting. Trick Daddy had a song

(Sugar) that he put out where he had candy references in the video, so I didn't go that route, and we tried to do something a little different… I'm really excited; I can't wait to see how the general public embraces my album. I'm just ready now; I've sat already long enough, almost 2 years."

50 hadn't exactly been sitting around. In addition to building his record label, which the rapper displayed a fantastically realistic attitude about in the context of longevity, despite G-Unit Records' wildly successful first year out, 50 reasoned—with impressive business acumen—that "you know, it's difficult enough to have the proper staffing, it's not easy to have knowledgeable people and it's expensive. And you need to have connections so you gotta come with the money."

"So, independently, when you come out, you can't just jump into that seat and then become a major. Look at majors as National Saving Banks. They got the money in order to allow you to create new projects. And the more success you have with them, the more finance they'll give you. When you do a subsidiary they kinda give you a 50 percent profit split and what that is they'll give you the money to make the project, cover the expenses to actually create the product and after they get their money back and you split the profits. So if you took yourself away from that, you have to have all the money upfront to make the record, to market it, all the money to transport the artists flying, hotels, cabs, limousines and you need to pay your staff at the same time."

"I mean, I'll be a major. I think G-Unit ain't Interscope records, it's just 2 years old, and Interscope is 13 years old." What made the triple-threat of Dre, Em and 50 work on a corporate and commercial level, according to Eminem, was a team strategy in which "Dre is the coach and I'm playing quarterback and 50 is the receiver, he's the go-to man right now. Everyone is set up in a place to play that position and it's more important for us to win overall, you know. It's about winning the championship as opposed to any individual getting the fame."

Consistent with his parent company's monopolistic business plan, 50 Cent has no intention of slowing down in 2005 following the March release of "St. Valentine's Day Massacre...(Then) I go to shoot my movie in April for 10 weeks...(In terms of the movie), we tailor-fit it. It's loosely based on my life story. It's difficult...Think about your life story. No matter how your life is, it's difficult to pick out what points you need to put in a two-hour film. You have to take your overall situation and create a story that kind of describes the best description of your life. You don't want to put people to sleep. The script is so good."

"I'm excited. For me it's more of a challenge than the music. I've already proven to myself that my ideas work....Then I have the soundtrack for the film, then Tony Yayo and Olivia's albums are being released, then Lloyd Banks and Young Buck's albums will be coming out in the fourth quarter alongside my video game I got with Universal for Bulletproof which is their answer to Grand Theft Auto. I got a book deal and a deal with Garcia Vitamin Water for Formula 50."

Still ever the hustler, 50 reasoned that "having this music, having Tony Yayo on deck and ready to go, following my album, after having Game sell 586,933 his first week, I'm anticipating selling even more than that my first week and then Yayo could possibly make more than that too, we're going uphill right now...Shortly after (my album's release in March), you'll see the first female solo artist of G-Unit, Olivia...I feel like I'm gonna have the biggest year in my career possibly this year." Addressing the topic of longevity, 50 explained that "I've always wanted to be happy and in peace. It's not always an option."

"Where I'm from we meet aggression with aggression. The kid in the schoolyard that doesn't want to fight always leaves with a black eye. If you allow them to walk over you, you invite them to do it more. Then you're subject to something even worse than you just going into the beef to begin with. That's just the way it is. Would I like not to have beef? Yeah. I'd like to just make music. Their beef is I make music better than them at this point."

"Maybe it'll decrease with time. Maybe when I retire. I have no intention of retiring. I'd like to make music until I can't make music anymore. Ain't gonna be no 50 Cent like Jay-Z retiring. I'm like LL… I'm going to be here until no one shows up. I love it too much." With mentors behind him like Eminem and Dr. Dre, both of whom have achieved the status of cultural icon, maintained their own artistic success commercially and critically, and in the same time, built respective business empires, 50 Cent looks as a student to Dre and Em continually as he makes his own rise in the latter categories, explaining that "I learned to be more patient (from Eminem and Dr. Dre)."

"I always want to do as much as I can. They're more perfectionists. Sometimes over-perfectionists. When you get like that, out of habit you start to second, third and fourth guess what you thinking. For me, it's like I get it and I go, this is right. That's it. Let's go. I've been able to have success doing that. When I start second guessing myself I think I'm ruining it. It's not organic anymore, not natural. I can't say lines like, 'I love you like a fat kid loves cake' when I'm dead serious. I've got to be enjoying myself or I won't come up with it, creatively…"

"People have disliked me since I can remember. It's just more people like me now than people who dislike me. More people know of me. Everyone's a judge…everyone's a critic. Everybody who bought a CD can criticize me. Now when people say I don't like 50 Cent they don't know me enough to not like me. Say you don't like the music. Say it's too aggressive. I break it down for them the way it is, the way I came up. When I make a record and I think I can't make a better record, I'll stop. That's the significance when Jay-Z says, 'What More Can I Say'."

Of course, 50 had much more to say, not just on his new album, but regarding his own future as he—through his success—has gained new perspective from the top of the mountain looking back down at all he's overcome in the course of his remarkable career thus far in the game. As fans, we've just seen the periphery of his ambition, because 50 is realizing his own potential in real time with his listeners. What we can expect from 50 Cent in the future depends on what his own expectations are for success in the rap game, and beyond.

The rapper seems focused on expanding his empire into the outward expanses of entrepreneurism now available to him, thanks in part to the blueprint invented by hip-hop mogul forefathers like Russell Simmons, Suge Knight and Sean 'P-Diddy' Combs, inherited and reinvented by Master P, Jay-Z and Damon Dash, and currently—in its third generation—being plied by the likes of Eminem, Dr. Dre and 50 Cent in its most refined and precise application.

50 Cent is taking aggressive advantage of the capital his initial success in 2003 earned him, seeking to pave new roads with his own stable of artists, and by breeding new superstars under the G-Unit brand, become a household name in hip-hop for generations to come. With personal net earnings for 2003/2004 topping the $50 Million mark and a # 1 debut on March 8th, 2005 for his sophomore album with a first-week soundscan tally well above 800,000 and counting, Curtis Jackson, a.k.a. 50 Cent is well on his way.

Ironically, according to 50 Cent, "(Five years ago), I really didn't (think I would be here.) I created a plan. I think everyone should have one. A five-year plan that you may shorten. You make short-term goals leading to your long-term goals. What happened to me was the success of Get Rich Or Die Tryin' sped up my five-year plan to a frame of about six months. I was able to maneuver everything else after those opportunities were provided for me because I had thought ahead. It wasn't like I was stuck."

"My first album, I said G-Unit, we in here. I was anticipating developing G-Unit into a record company. A lot of people view us as a group and as I begin to diversify the kind of music that comes from our camp, they'll start to appreciate us more as a company...I'm not ever gonna retire. I'm only dropping my second album; I'm so early in my career. Because my first album was such a big success, people start asking 'when you're gonna retire?' But I'm not even thinking about that, I'm more in the mind frame 'when do I come out again."

"I don't even care (about bootlegging). My deal itself—I'm in a good space financially, you know? As long as it's being heard, those people are the people that are supporting me at the concerts. Right now I've been touring, won the mixed tape circuit. I think the mixed tape circuit is the largest form of promotion. The bootlegger is just trying to feed his family, it's not going to stop. Don't ever think it's gonna stop—It's a hustle. They hustlin' to get their money, you can't beat 'em. You might as well just capitalize off of them, and that's what I did in the beginning with the mixed tapes circuit."

—50 Cent

Chapter 7
The Mix Tape Circuit

There's nothing funny about bootlegging… It costs the industry and artists millions of dollars a year in lost sales revenue. It makes it inherently harder for labels to allot budget to signing as many new bands as they used to, constricting the chance for the market to be as artistically competitive and vibrant as it has been in years past. Bootlegging as a business is as cutthroat as the crack game, and unlike downloading, its NEVER free. Fans still pay, the only ones who get shortchanged financially are the artists and labels.

The traditional response to bootlegging and downloading, i.e. music piracy, has been lawsuits, and in the case of bootlegging, street raids by law enforcement. And much like the drug trade, when the cops do hit paydirt and bust a bootlegging ring, the impact on the overall business is minimal at best, and hardly preventative. With the introduction of the mix tape phenomenon in New York in the early millennium, a different strategy for dealing with bootlegging emerged, that of 'If You Can't Beat Em, Join Em.'

Rather than fight the inevitable spread of bootleg recordings, established rappers for all intents and purposes went into business with their former adversaries, essentially making 'authorized bootlegs', non-label sanctioned studio recordings that featured established performers among a sea of the best in up and coming New York underground hip hop.

Among the very first emcees to embrace this business model was 50 Cent, who, following his being dropped from Columbia in 2000, took it back to the streets to rebuild his career and reputation. Recording dozens of independently produced rap tracks, 50 then released full-length bootleg albums, with original artwork, that had NEVER been released conventionally into retail to begin with.

Seen by hip hop fans on the same streetcorner blankets for sale alongside Jay-Z, Nas, Biggie Smalls and Tupac Shakur, 50 got a buzz going that was unique to anything that the industry had witnessed before. In fact, aside from the aforementioned Shakur, who, aside from remaining hip hop's biggest catalog seller, is also the best selling bootleg artist in the trade, due principally to the posthumous release of much of the 150 tracks he recorded but never released during the last 8 months of his life.

As such, when the larger hip hop community—including mainstream (i.e. suburban) fans, and record executives who had seen the money being made on the street level and immediately wanted a piece—caught on and started paying close attention to who were the hottest sellers in the underground market, instead of finding established names at the top of the list, they found a virtual unknown.

In fact, up to the point that the bidding war first broke out over 50 in 2002, his only mention on MTV News.com had been an article about his shooting in 2000. Completely circumventing the majors, 50 and his mixtape counterparts had also innovated the traditional street model of selling records out of a car trunk. The Mix Tape circuit was far more organized, set up much like a drug sales model—one principle supplier with lots of independent dealers set up on street corners in neighborhoods around New York, from the Bronx through Manhattan and all the way in to the farthest reaches of Brooklyn and Queens.

The distribution network was impressive, but not surprising to anyone familiar with ghetto entrepreneurship as it had traditionally related to drug dealing, gambling, or related African American-controlled illicit activities in the inner city. Blacks had their own mafia just like the Italians and Irish did, and it was sophisticated to the point that it went largely unnoticed to the culturally biased federal government, who had cast African Americans in the Black Panther Movement and underestimated their ability to civilly get over on the system.

The only difference in the mix tape circuit was that, technically, mix tapes themselves were legal, despite the largely illegal bootlegging distribution system they were a part of. Once the spotlight fell on mix tapes, the industry quickly figured the latter out, and sought to become that much more involved on the street level. Of course, the ultimate goal was to sweep up the hottest underground talent in the process, but the street entrepreneurs still kept tight reign on the whole enterprise as it related to production and distribution.

The only advertising was word of mouth, and so the overhead was limited to the cost of recording and manufacturing the mix tape CD's. In the case of artists like 50, who released entire albums of material via the mix tape circuit vs. appearing in one-offs on compilation albums featuring a variety of up and coming emcees, he made direct deals with the distributors, typically making as much as $3 per album for himself, a profit margin well above the average major label rap record deal. As the rapper explained, "you know what? Through the mixtape circuit I actually put out a album independently and it did well. 'Guess Who's Back' was the highest selling independent album."

As MTV explained in an exclusive special on the phenomenon of mix tapes amidst 50's nuclear rise to the top, "What exactly are mix tapes? In the days of old (the '70s) they were exactly what they were called: Cassette tapes with a mix of music from different artists put together by a DJ. Before rap records were even made, such DJs as Grandmaster Flash, Kool Herc and Afrika Bambaataa would record their party-spinning and performances at clubs and sell the tapes in the streets for $20 a pop."

"These days, mixtapes come primarily as CDs, cost $5 to $10, and can feature any or all of the following: Sought-after, unreleased 'exclusive' tracks and previously released songs from A-list or up-and-coming rappers; Freestyles—an artist rhyming for one or two verses over one of their peers' beats; An entire 'unofficial' album from one artist; DJs' special mixes of songs or the blending of two different tracks together; Turntablists and artists speaking out on current topics affecting themselves or the hip-hop community; and DJs playing popular collections of songs at considerably slower speeds than normal..."

"All of this happens with little to no involvement from record labels... Artists say the purity of the music on mixtapes can be matched by packaging that is unflinching as well. 'There are certain things that major (labels) won't allow us to do 'cause they don't feel like it's acceptable for marketing a project,' 50 Cent explained. 'Like they haven't allowed a gun on the cover of a CD since (Boogie Down Productions') Criminal Minded (and By All Means Necessary), but those guns are still in the 'hood. So when I did the marketing for some of my street projects, I used things that were a little edgier than what they would use at the majors right now. I got a chance to express myself in a different way'....So how do mixtapes actually get to the street? Once the DJs or rhymers have assembled their underground offering, it's not shipped to Wal-Mart, Virgin or FYE. This part of the mixtape game even the most vocal of record spinners don't like to talk about. And if you do get them to speak on it, without batting an eye they'll tell you they have nothing to do with how their product gets out to consumers..."

"Word on the street says that some DJs sell mixtapes to the stores either on consignment or straight-up for between $3 and $6 apiece, then the store will sell them for upwards of $10. Some DJs will sell their mixtapes to a 'wholesaler' who presses up mass quantities of CDs. A wholesaler might also buy a CD at a store and then copy it himself. The wholesaler will sell it to the vendors on the streets for anywhere from $1.50 to $3—it all depends on how hot the mixtape is..."

"While West Coast artists seem to prefer direct selling of complete albums, and the Atlanta scene focuses on basic party mixtapes, other areas of the U.S. are catching on. DJ Mike Love is holding it down in Chicago, and his Midwest neighbors, the St. Lunatics, are planning to put out their own mixtapes and help the St. Louis scene thrive. Meanwhile, Lil' Wayne and his new group, the Squad, have been generating a heavy buzz in New Orleans. Not to mention all the DJs who put out their mixtapes on the Internet. Given the story of 50 Cent, it seems likely that mixtape mania will only spread across the rest of the country."

Back home in New York, the establishment had already been paying attention to the buzz 50 was generating a full year before he even was brought to the attention of Eminem, back in 2001. As rapper Jay-Z commented at that time on 50's rise in the NY hip hop underground, "Right now, maybe not all over the world but in New York, (50 Cent) has the streets on fire."

In 50's eyes, the mix tape circuit was like bootcamp for up and coming rappers, and a perfect litmus test for major labels seeking to see how the street is responding to a new record, by a new or established artist, among a host of other advantages for the industry at large, "(mix tapes are) like entry level hip-hop. Once you go in the studio, and record a record that you think is a hit, you've got to test it. So, you put it on a mixtape. Your A-class mixtape DJs are DJs that have radio airplay."

"The B-class DJs have the most stores and your C-class DJs are your local mixtape DJs. Once your A-class DJs put a record on their mixtape and they get a (good) response, they play it on the radio. I think that's the most effective marketing tool. Once you generate enough interest for the bootleggers to bootleg a CD, I think you should have them bootleg your CD to the point where it's excessive."

"It only hurts an established artist to be bootlegged. It hurts you if your album is old shit or if your record is wack...and it gets out that (your album's) not hot...(For a new artist though), once the tape is out and its hot, or you have a buzz around you big enough, every bootlegger will have it...I think people purchase that to hear what's hot and what's new, and I was able to market myself the way I wanted to market myself. If I wanted to put a gun on a CD it's OK...You know you're album is gonna come out 2 weeks before it come out, (so there's) no way to get around the bootlegs...I think, the bootleggers, I think mix tapes are like black market distribution, I think bootleggers are effective for new artists."

"Once they get a buzz strong enough for them to bootleg them, they can circulate music to the point that they become popular. So I distribute my music through there to the point where they understand that buying a 50 cent record is a safe buy, you not gonna have to question whether there's going to be quality material on there or not cuz you heard him before." Roc-A-Fella Records CEO Damon Dash echoed 50 on the importance of the mix tape circuit in the areas of establishing credibility and buzz, explaining "that's the way we got our fame and the way we got our word-of-mouth on the streets…That's the best way to talk to that real hip-hop consumer. That's how you get your respect. If you're a real rapper, you don't have to make a record for the radio or something for MTV. You get to really showcase your skills on mixtapes. We're always gonna use that as a tool."

As 50's reputation on the mixtape circuit spread like wildfire across New York, the phenomenon itself was beginning a national exposure that would turn the industry on its head, and it was no surprise when the press began to pay attention to 50 that he had been one of the artistic pioneers of the latest innovation in hip hop marketing. Inextricably linked to the mix tape movement, 50 Cent became America's hottest rapper because he was the country's hottest underground rapper.

As far as 50 himself felt about being labeled as rap's next big thing, he explained that by coming up through the mix tape circuit, he also remained largely grounded to what was going on around 50 with his career commercially, "I'm excited about my whole scenario right now…I also think it's sustained off the consistency. I've been putting music out. That would make sense, you know? Because first it's like they ain't lookin' at pluggin' you. It's just like, 'Get that record away.' But I make music for the mixtapes because it's important. I feel like that's the largest form of promotion… I think you gotta stay consistent, consistency is the key to all success. So I stay in the studio and make music constantly!"

Even after he'd signed his deal with Eminem and Dr. Dre, 50 continued to faithfully release music via the underground, thanks to a clause in his contract that allowed him to. From 50's vantage point, even on top, it was the only certain way to stay fresh with fans, such that , as the rapper explained, "(Its) a business angle…I saturate the street market…We do a mixtape for everything we do, put it right on the street. We always put out a mixtape 'cause you gotta keep your presence in the street. (Fans) start to doubt you…if you don't consistently keep something hot in front of them. So I keep it out there."

Concerning the rapper's views on music piracy overall, once he was in the position to become rap's best selling artist, and its most downloaded online, 50 remained surprisingly, or not, supportive of the whole trade, "I don't have a problem with (downloading). I think…people were tried of being cheated, by music, by buying albums that have one good record two good records, I think they are checking. I think that even people who download music will go out and buy the CD, after they hear it and hear a lot of good music on it…"

"Bootleggin can be used a form of promotion.. Like when you create a buzz for your stuff, I have no beef with bootleggin…I mean when people hear good music, that's when they buy the CD anyway! And I think when people buy bootlegs, they buy it cause they got cheated! I think they download it, cause in the past they bought CDs that maybe had 8 cuts…Once they hear you enough to know that you're gone get them a good record, they gone end up spendin money on your CD…"

"Right now my whole show is somebody else's show and I'm runnin around probably getting more they getting to perform right now, that's crazy. It feels good—my momentum is…worth all of the other stuff that happenin'…It feels so good like when I go out in the club, and it's five thousand, 3500 people there and they know every word to the song. That's why I'm not mad at the bootleggers, cause when they know it I mean at least they got it as long as I'm reaching the people. Even if they don't buy this record, they'll buy the next one. They'll feel like, 'You know what I'm gonna get that and it's worth me spending my 15 or 16 dollars', so it don't even matter to me. They gonna get it, eventually they'll catch up catch onto it and buy it—you can't stop it anyway."

MTV News validated 50's belief that mix tapes are often preferred by consumers where available to traditional retail, explaining in their mix tape expo that "Right now, mixtapes are still most popular where they started, in the streets of New York, where they're sold (illegally, as no taxes are collected and samples aren't cleared) in mom-and-pop stores and on blankets alongside black-market copies of popular current albums. And in the battle of legitimate albums versus mixtapes, mixtapes are increasingly the winners… At a time when the 'real' music business is crumbling—sales figures last year were down 8.7 percent from 2001—the mixtape industry is thriving. For one thing, the mixtapes are cheaper than regular albums on sale at retail outlets. And fans know when they get their hands on a mixtape, most of the tracks are probably going to be hot."

Once 50 started blowing up, and the mix tape industry along with him, the industry at large quickly went about saturating and generifying the market on a nation-wide level. And while 50 would play the majors' game to promote the release of his debut album under his deal with Em and Dre, the emcee still made sure to stay local, where trends were made before they ever caught on nationally, and where artists who hung around in the game at large kept their roots, "I'm never gonna give up my presence in the streets, because without that I wouldn't have the opportunities to do what I'm doing now…I can't allow that. That's my core base, so if that's gone I don't think I'll exist long. It might be one day (the masses) decide, 'Oh 50's not hot no more, this other guy is,' and I'm gone."

"If your original base is not there, how do you expect to stay?…A new artist on the system that's designed by the majors, all you'll know from them (before you buy their album) is that very first single that they decide to put out…There's been several artists before that have released CDs that had only one good song or two good songs and that's what causes people not to purchase CDs immediately. They wait until they find out if this guy gives up a quality performance all the time. By then, your sales go down. Rap changes so rapidly that they can decide what you did for that album isn't hot anymore. I felt like I had to take advantage of that opportunity and hit the streets with the music myself…The mixtapes are like me speaking directly to my neighborhood."

As 50's rise to the top of hip hop began, in addition to having the underground credibility with the streets via the mix tape circuit, the instant commercial credibility via his alliance with Eminem and Dr. Dre, he also had the one thing that any great hip hop icon must have in order to embody living controversy as a part of his persona, the all important BEEF. And boy did 50 have one, with a poorly matched adversary granted, but still with a rapper who had a name, guaranteeing that the media would pay immediate attention. 50's beef with Ja Rule extended back to 2000, prior to his shooting, which later heightened speculation that Murder Inc.-affiliate Kenneth 'Supreme'

McGriff had played a role in ordering and orchestrating the attempt on 50's life. That 50 had survived, trashed Ja Rule thereafter for 2 years on the mix tape circuit, and now had the back up he did with Em and Dre in facing Murder Inc., whose commercial peak had already come, it was a battle stacked in 50's favor. On authenticity alone, 50 Cent was immediately superior to Ja Rule, who had largely made his name via duets on love ballads with R&B singers like Ashanti and J-Lo.

In a song called 'Wanksta', which 50 wrote exclusively about Ja Rule, and released to the streets a full year before it was included on the '8 Mile' Soundtrack and became 50's first commercial hit record, Ja took an immediate hit. Clearly out of his league, along with his record label, Irv Gotti and the Murder Inc. posse did NOT execute a clear and concise response to 50's brutal attack on Ja Rule's character and credibility as an emcee as 2003 unfolded. For 50, it was revenge, for Ja Rule, it was sad and embarrassing, and would put a permanent in his already struggling career…

"You're a poptart sweetheart, you're soft in the middle...
and your boss is a bitch, if he could he would,
sell his soul for cheap tricks, like to be Suge
you can buy cars, but can't by respect in the hood
maybe I'm so disrespectful, cause to me you're a mystery
I know niggas from your hood, you have no history
never nothin', never popped nothin', nigga stop frontin',
Jay put you on, X made you hot,
now you run around like you're some big shot—PUSSY"

—50 Cent on Ja Rule and Murder Inc. boss Irv Gotti, "Back Down"

Chapter 8

Wanksta—50 Cent Vs. Ja Rule, Irv Gotti and Murder Inc.

Shit talking is a part of the rap game. As with any competitive sport, without trash talking there wouldn't be a real spirit of rivalry, and where most of hip hop's ghosts have sadly become such as a result of the aforementioned rivalries—cases in point being the Notorious BIG and Tupac—in the case of the beef between 50 Cent and Ja Rule, no such extremity was anticipated, on 50's part anyway.

Though federal authorities speculate that a Murder Inc. silent partner, Kenneth 'Supreme' McGriff, may have been responsible for ordering the attempt on 50's life, that he had survived the ordeal only emboldened him in his quest to take hip hop's top spot. Aiding him in his crusade was the support network, both corporate and among his peers, and most importantly in the streets, that 50 had behind him, but also the fact that the opposition he had before him—that being Ja Rule and Murder Inc.—was a literal joke.

Ja Rule was 5'1, weighed 110 pounds, and had no street credibility of his own to speak of, outside that of his label's phantom owner, Kenneth 'Supreme' McGriff, who had taken his shot at 50 and missed. Therein, 50's attitude toward any sort of threat that Ja Rule may have posed him was lighthearted, i.e. he didn't take it seriously when coming from Ja Rule's mouth. Perhaps this was in part because for as much trash as Ja Rule spewed from one side of his mouth, out of the other he sang love song duets with the likes of Jennifer Lopez and Ashanti.

To 50, Ja Rule talking tough was comical, such that, "I think he's a clown, all he's missin is a red nose, a wig, and the shoes." With the rise of 50 Cent, rap was experiencing a new age of authenticity, a genuine reinvention of the gangsta presence in hip hop, reminiscent of the Death Row heyday. Where 50 could rap about being shot or dealing drugs and back it up with Emergency Room lawsuits and criminal rapsheets, Ja Rule is a studio gangster, flat out, with no one to back up any claims to the contrary.

Ja Rule went to desperate lengths from the starting gate to convince the hip hop world that he was on 50's thug level, going as far as to falsify an NYPD restraining order on Hot 97, which 50, and the rest of the industry, found as laughable as the notion that Ja Rule was on 50's level, "Seven days before his album drops he goes to radio says I have an order of protection on him…c'mon, (Ja Rule) weighs 110 pounds wet, and with his pockets full of change." Certainly not when he felt he had to sink that low.

Moreover, Murder Inc.'s attempts to paint themselves as 'the most dangerous record label in the world' had sputtered to almost an immediate halt when Ja Rule became a back-up singer for the industry's biggest female R&B divas. An unforgivable contradiction in street terms, a rapper's back-up, or 'back' in urban slang, is almost as important to securing his credibility and authority as his own ability as a leading man to command it. To think Tupac and Suge, who immortalized the model in the course of the East Coast/West Coast beef, and set the mold historically for future hip hop generations to follow.

Toward that end, Irv Gotti had attempted a short cut in this race, aligning himself with Suge Knight in the hopes of gaining instant gangsta credibility by mere affiliation, which might have been a golden move in Death Row's hey day. Still, while Suge was as feared as ever throughout the industry following his release from prison in late 2001, it wasn't anymore because his label was a force in hip hop, but simply because Suge was a living legend, the last man standing for everything that thug life was meant to represent as an active force in rap.

Much of it had died with Tupac and Biggie, and the remnants were unwelcomed in the years that followed, as hip hop regrouped, entered the bling bling era, and went through its first real commercial explosion as a corporate entity. Where Columbia had not been ready for 50 Cent the first time around, he was returned to the underground, while watered-down versions of gangster rappers like Ja Rule, Mase, and Ludacris were pushed by major labels into the mainstream as the popular norm.

For Irv Gotti to attempt to kickstart the true thug era of hip hop back to life by hanging out with its founder simply wouldn't work because he had nothing to build on, and every great has a foundation. Murder Inc. couldn't stand on its own based on the public faces the label had chosen to represent it in the streets, and certainly couldn't openly reveal what authentic criminal affiliations it did have via Kenneth 'Supreme' McGriff because that would have made Irv Gotti's corporate backers nervous.

Where Suge Knight had strong-armed his way into the business, owning his masters from the outset, Def Jam/Island Records owned Murder Inc., so in reality Gotti was not truly calling his own shots. Much like Sean 'P. Diddy' Combs' joint-venture deal with Arista had stipulated, if Gotti was convicted of a felony of any sort that prohibited him from actively running his label, control and ownership in essence would revert to his corporate partners. Knight had not had this problem when he faced incarceration, both because he owned his catalog and therein controlled his destiny, but more importantly because he wasn't therein beholden to anyone, and could afford to keep it real because he had done so from the outset.

Suits knew what to expect with Suge, and dealt with him anyway because he kept the money rolling in as a direct result of his label's lifestyle. Conversely, Murder Inc. had come out of the starting gate with an inherently cleaner image, and while the label's stars excelled at ghetto theatrics, doing photo shoots and videos dressed in 1930's style gangster garb and even driving antique cars from the era, behind the curtain corporate executives were carefully holding the strings.

Ja Rule and Irv Gotti may have been entertaining, but their gangster portrayal was just that, entertainment. Art definitely did NOT imitate life when it came to Ja Rule and Murder Inc., and fans knew it, letting it slide because the industry had largely gone soft in the absence of the sort of legitimate authenticity Tupac, Biggie and Death Row had brought to the game.

Perhaps most importantly, for rap fans, where Suge Knight was a gangsta, Irv Gotti was not. Knight had spent years under Federal investigation for racketeering, openly sported his gang colors, and had been incarcerated in a maximum security prison for the second half of the 1990s, reinforcing and cementing his legacy as the most authentic gangsta in hip hop. For Gotti to believe that he could simply side up to Knight in the media and achieve the sort of instant credibility the Death Row endorsement once secured was naive.

The translation between thug life and guaranteed platinum record sales had been defunct for years, as dead as Tupac or Biggie. Both because Death Row had passed its heyday, and because Suge was now his label's biggest star, rebuilding his artist roster and commercial viability outside of catalog releases from scratch, Gotti had miscalculated the return he would get from investing himself in a public affiliation with Knight. Especially when Gotti's adversary was considered—50 Cent, backed by Eminem and Dr. Dre commercially, and Interscope corporately.

While Suge had built Interscope via Death Row's sales, and given Dr. Dre the opportunity to become a mogul in his own right, Knight was a true independent, and enjoyed walking his own path, often in a spirit of defiance that was long lost on hip hop as a whole. And where Suge had, historically, always relished the opportunity to involve himself in or escalate any controversy that would sell records, it had always been with the stipulation that he would benefit financially in the process.

This time around, Suge did not have a Tupac or Snoop Dogg to pit against a rival, nor could he afford to personally, as his freedom was still controlled by the California Department of Corrections. Simply, Gotti's beef was not Suge's, nor did Knight seemed overly interested in involving himself in the beef that ensued between 50 Cent's camp and Gotti's, perhaps having had his fill with Tupac and Biggie, or not wanting to fight Gotti's battles for him.

50 had already gone against all odds, and won, but it had been a while since hip hop had anything in the way of a tangible all-star beef, so fans were willing to sit back and watch the show, and it was as entertaining to them as it was to 50 himself, given the free publicity, and the fact that he did legitimately hate Ja Rule, "it's different…when it's on wax it stays on wax, when it's something else, it's not really wax. Me and (Ja) don't get along period. You

know what I mean? It is what it is. To expand on it, I mean he will say anything out of his mouth to try and get attention. Like I mean he ain't a 110 pounds with change in his pockets soaking wet, and still make like 'I need a lot of protection from him', it's crazy, but I couldn't pay for the promotions—(its) priceless."

Following the eruption of the beef between Ja Rule and 50, Irv Gotti and Co. did anything they could to inflame and escalate the rivalry, in hopes that it would restart their faltering engines and boost slagging record sales. While this strategy worked in 50's favor, Ja Rule's career would be irrevocably damaged, and from 50's vantage point, he viewed Ja Rule as basically "obsessed with me…I couldn't pay for that kind of promotion! He goes everywhere, his whole radio tour—I mean it's obvious that nobody cares about his Ja Rule record in the 'hood."

"In the street, there's no heat; his new record sucks, period. Like, you can't keep doing the same thing. If you don't step up and make better music, you just going to fade, you'll go away. And his format, like his pop thing that he's doing, it's obvious he would like to sell records like 50 Cent sells records. He would like to be me if he could. As a matter of fact, he wouldn't want to be me, he would like to be DMX or Tupac, you know what I'm saying? That's who he would like to be, but he would like to sell records the way that they sell records, and the way I sell records is closer to that than what he's doing. And it bothers him."

Perhaps 50's biggest criticism of Ja Rule was of his status as a studio gangsta, a style of rap which insulted 50's most basic sense of authenticity, based on what he had been through in his life, and built his reputation as an emcee upon, "There's a lot (of studio gangsters), I think that 90% of the population in hip-hop…I don't believe them. Until I see them go through situations I ain't gonna believe it… To me, rappers are liars until I see that their actions coincide with what they said through the music…Like, you got people running around calling themselves murderers. I don't know murderers that call themselves murderers."

"I don't know none of them that do that. I know people that kill people who've done it before and will do it now if placed in that situation, but I don't know them to call themselves murderers…I always looked at Ja like he's a weak little shit. He's never been in any of the tough-guy scenarios he raps about. He grew up a Jehovah's Witness, the motherfucker that knocks on your door on Saturday and tries to sell you a Watchtower. Meanwhile I was hustling to provide for myself. He's not strong enough or smart enough to maintain anything…What makes him envy me is, I can sell records the way he would like to sell records. People don't wanna hear that story from him. He jumping around on TV too long in the rain with Mary J. Blige."

As 50 explains the root of the beef from his perspective, "It started cuz, I know someone, a friend of mine robbed him, and after he robbed him (Ja) saw me in the club, you know we was kicking it, he saw me kicking it with the kid that robbed him and he feel like he wasn't saying anything to the kid that robbed him, but he felt like he could treat me differently cuz im supposed to be like his peer because we both rap…So after (he) got robbed, (he was) like, our 'hood ain't that big. I know somebody that robbed him and we was in a club and I say, 'What's up? I'm kicking it with the kid regular (who robbed Ja).' (So Ja asks) 'You know him?', (I say) 'Yeah, I know him. You know I'm not going to (bring up with him that) he robbed you. That's your business. If you're going to deal with him, deal with him. As a matter of fact, you not saying anything to him—he's standing right here.'"

"And (Ja) didn't say nothing to the kid but he treats me differently, like he's upset with me for kicking it with the kid. Or he don't want to associate with me 'cause I associate with the people that did something to him. I just think that when you become a rapper, other rappers feel like you're their peer. And everybody ain't been through the same thing, the things you been through make up who you are. Everybody's not the same, but because you rap, there could be somebody out there in the 'hood doing

whatever, and as soon as they decide to rap, a rapper can be standing in your face and say anything to you—whatever he wrote in
his rhyme, say it in your face like he mean it, knowing that he ain't
going to do nothing that he say in that rhyme."

"Like, he ain't never did none of that and ain't going to do none of
that. And that's the part of me moving from the street to music
that I had—I had a bumpy road to go down, 'cause I was still dealing with my morals from the street and the music thing." Things
escalated thereafter when, in March, 2000, Ja and 50 ran into one
another again at the Hit Factory, a Manhattan recording studio,
and a scuffle ensued where it has been alleged that 50 was stabbed
in the lung and taken to the emergency room. Though no hospital
records or police reports exist to substantiate these allegations,
spread by the Murder Inc. PR machine, 50 personally has refuted
the extremity of the entire incident, explaining that "I ended up
getting three stitches. A nick...It was a scratch. It stopped bleed-
ing on its own."

"I went home, and my grandmother said, 'You should go to the
hospital—you could get an infection.' It was no big deal. They
expanded that shit to make it look good for them. I had already
punched this boy Ja Rule in the eye, in Atlanta...When they came
to the Hit Factory, they were truly blessed. If they had come about
10 minutes before, one of them would have been killed. Because
my jacket was in another room. You see what I'm saying?...I would
have tried to kill anybody that came in the room. In New York State
you're allowed to use the same force to protect yourself as a person is
using against you. So I'd have just started firing. Fuck it."

For Murder Inc.'s part, Irv Gotti and Ja Rule went on Hot 97,
claiming 50 had filed an order of protection against them, and
even producing what they alleged to be a copy of the order, which
The Source later proved to be a forgery. For 50's part, he emphati-
cally and comically denies the claim, explaining that "to my
knowledge it's not true. They could've done that shit, to make

themselves look hard. Me? I ain't going to a fucking police precinct to file an order of protection on these niggas. Look at this guy—he's a fucking idiot. Names himself Gotti. You know where the name Murder Inc. originates? This guy watches too many movies."

More significant however, was the fact that the scuffle with Irv Gotti and company preceded 50's shooting in May of that same year. While the attempted murder remains officially deemed an unsolved homicide, federal authorities investigating Murder Inc.'s ties to Kenneth 'Supreme' McGriff, suspect that McGriff was behind the shooting. Whether the assault on 50 was motivated, in whole or in part, out of the beef with Murder Inc. remains in question. The coincidence is suspect, especially when considering the ties between McGriff and Murder Inc., still it could have been drug related, given 50's occupation at the time.

For 50's part, he has stayed largely neutral on whether McGriff was behind the shooting, confirming only that "the cops thought he was responsible for me getting shot." Regardless, there is clearly no love lost between the two, further supporting the theory that McGriff was in fact involved in orchestrating the hit on 50. The rapper sums his relationship with McGriff up as simply one in which "we just don't get along. Fuck him. I was saying that before he went to jail. He don't like me, neither. He let niggas say shit about me that he was supposed to check at the gate. He was letting niggas call me a snitch."

"Where I'm from, you sentence a nigga to death by calling him a snitch…(As far as whether he had me set up in that shooting), I don't know for sure. But I hate to talk about this shit now. If people ask me those questions, the police are going to feel, Well, we should bring him in and ask him some questions. And I don't have anything to say to the police. For me, when the cops come, it's to take me away. So what does that do to me? That puts me in contempt of court, and they got me in jail. McGriff is a fucking loser. He had a strong fucking crew that would do anything, kill anything. But everybody affiliated with him is in the penitentiary or dead. That's the kind of leader he is."

With McGriff in prison on a parole violation by the time that 50 and Ja Rule's beef took center stage in the hip hop media, 50 already seemed to have the upper hand in the battle, both in terms of record sales, and in terms of the public opinion on who was the weaker adversary. 50 took every opportunity he could in the beginning to smash on Ja Rule, taking shots at his street credibility and commercial viability whenever he could, reasoning with one journalist that "I dislike what happened to Ja Rule…It's like he's not strong enough to stand on his own in any situation."

"Right now he's…terrified, without the support of people he would have around, he's gonna be lost. See I've been on my own so I'm comfortable, you know what I mean? In (street) situations, and (Ja) ain't gonna be comfortable in that situation…When you get in a point when you generate finances in a circle of people, they gonna treat you like as if you're gonna bring the money— you're the cash cow, so they ain't gonna disrespect you. They gonna treat you like you one of the crew…But in all actuality, you haven't been in the trenches (which Ja hasn't), you haven't done any of the things that these guys did."

"(Now), (Ja) need them around in order for people to go 'Naw don't do that to him, cuz homeboy be holdin him down, cuz this guy is cool with them.' But it's never because of you, you see what I'm sayin? I think (Ja's) kinda got pushed over into that situation…I think that happened to him." In breaking down what was fake about Ja's crew, 50 broadens his attack, reasoning that "you're John Gotti boy, you like fancy suits, you want people to notice you when you go to the clubs you want to do everything else and you go down like John Gotti go down when you do that…(But) gangsters behind the scene don't say nothing, they keep putting in work, they gonna keep doin it."

"You see what I'm sayin?...Ja Rule, that boy is not makin me sell records and now he's actually on the down spiral, he's goin down. All that lollipop—him and Ashanti is damn near a group, this is the second duet they did together. (That ain't street!)" One laughable and critical error on Ja Rule's part was to come out against not only 50 Cent, but also Eminem and Dre, suggesting in one interview that if "If you're gonna be authorizing (50 Cent) to spew records on me, then I wanna do what I gotta do to take your company under. And that goes for Dre, Em or whoever."

Not only was Ja Rule in ANY position commercially to inflict such damage, while 50, and certainly Eminem and Dr. Dre, were, but Murder Inc. also, having past the peak of its 15 minutes of fame, wasn't in a position to reinforce Ja Rule's attempts in any credible fashion. 50 went as far as to not only call Ja Rule a studio gangster and a fraud, but also took the time to explain why, breaking down Ja's role playing into the following analysis, "Sometimes when you're in a situation where you generate finances for everybody around you, the people around you make (you) feel like (you're) everything, 'You're the hottest thing period.'"

"As an artist, you're moving around, doing shows, doing alot of things, you can start to believe you're all that counts...Ja's desperate at this point, because...he came out...in magazines saying if Em and Dre co-sign 50, that he's gonna destroy their companies...(Ja) overlooked the fact that Dr. Dre has been successful all this time since N.W.A., (and) Eminem's success is phenomenal... I felt, Im trippin, Im excited about him being so stupid you know? You would think with person having that type of success that they would have to at least have some type of business sense...How about what he his first week, he did double the sixth week..."

"Theres no comparison, to (Ja) and Eminem. I don't even know where he sticks his mouth to say that where you get in a circle full of people who you provide for cuz there is, cuz he does generate money and you know what I mean? He's probably the strongest artist on Murder Inc. So that whole camp has to feel that he's the bread winner, so because of that, they will treat him like he's ill, like he has some pull in your own circle."

"What happens is you start to believe that then feel like you run shit, even making that statement, how can he stop any body from doing something, no body got to ask him to sign, it bothers him that 50 Cent is in position, he's intimidated. (Ja's sales ain't) no where near (Eminem's)…(Murder Inc. is) hurting, them niggas is bitches…(Ja's last record ain't selling, and) that's what fucking happens! He makes a whole fucking album where he's attacking me. You say something negative about me (or Em or Dre), people are not going to like you."

Regardless of the sides record buyers took in the beef, the commercial results reminded the industry, in the spirit of the Biggie vs. Tupac East Coast/West Coast war, that controversy sells! 50's label boss Eminem became a victim of the latter when he was attacked shortly after 50 by *The Source Magazine* co-owner and wanna-be rapper Ray Benzino, who most industry insiders and fans saw as a joke coming out of the gate. Ironically, both 50 and Eminem had weak opponents in common, and as a result, were more than happy to come to one another's defense, on diss records and in print media.

To 50, the controversy Benzino was attempting to stir up was transparent, and he called it for what it was right off—laughable, pointing out that "that's not beef, (Benzino dissing Eminem.)… That ain't no beef, that's Benzino taking a shot at Em trying to get some attention…(That) ho, he's reaching. I mean you know, you could have investments that work if your not content with your situation your always going to make a fool of yourself cuz your not happy with where your at. Like you got a company, he's a part owner of *The Source Magazine*, but that's not what he wants to be, he wants to be a hot rapper."

"So he give his own album 4 mikes, put himself on the cover, its crazy! He's probably the only rapper been on the cover of *The Source Magazine* that doesn't have a hit…2 pages ads in your own magazine, it's all good. It's not even something I got to say for them to figure out themselves. But that's about over right now Em's not putting any more energy or even going to respond to questions about Benzino…"

"When I first heard about that, I thought there was a situation where they like ran into each other, but they never ran into each other! Its just you know, Benzino is taking shots at Em cause he's doin' so well, hopin' it would give him some attention!…Yo, he's crazy. (But) that's not beef. That's a stunt, a promotional stunt. We have no altercations, no interaction and now we have beef? How?"

By the end of 2003, both Ja Rule & Co. and Benzino had lost their respective battles with 50 and Em—BADLY. The damage to both adversaries careers were severe, especially in Ja Rule's case. Fans had sided with 50 because he was a hotter emcee and the more credible of the two gangstas, period. Ja Rule was punished by fans for his assault too, as his record sales continue to decline, and his label loses steam by the day—in both the commercial and legal arenas.

By the end of the beef, 50 himself had tired of giving Ja Rule free press by discussing the controversy, explaining to one journalist that the question he most hated being asked in the media was "'What's the beef between you and Ja Rule?' My career is not based on Ja Rule. I put out so much music that entertains people and has nothing to do with him." In general, 50 felt beefs were healthy now and then for the rap industry, with the stipulation it be legitimate, explaining that "Hip-hop has always been competitive. (But) it depends on what type of beef it is. I don't get into rap beef for no reason."

"I don't jump on anyone because I don't like the way their last song sounded…(Beef is) effective (for selling records)…I just do what I do. I don't anticipate, I don't say, 'Yo, I'm not going to say this because this guy was talking about that guy and that guy was talking about this guy, so if I do that it's going to feel like this.' No, that's cosmetic. That means you're not going off your true feelings. If I'm upset about something, I write it. And if it happens to be a hit, then I'll put it on my record; other than that, it may be still be on the tape in the studio."

"If it's not a hit record at the end of the day, it's all good—I wouldn't pick my album based on I got to say something about somebody on my album. I think that's corny. If you really don't have an issue in you that's out there, that's wack. I understand if you bumped into someone or you have some differences somehow down the way that you really don't get along, cool. You got some shit to get off your chest, go ahead. But if you just picking somebody, that's not cool."

UNITED STATES DISTRICT COURT
EASTERN DISTRICT OF NEW YORK

03 0023M

- - - - - - - - - - - - - - - - - - - -X

IN RE SEIZURE OF ALL FUNDS HELD IN ALL
BANK ACCOUNTS MAINTAINED AT HSBC
BANK, INCLUDING, BUT NOT LIMITED TO
ACCOUNT NUMBERS 504-063405, 504-455273,
504-063413, 504-064487, IN THE NAME
OF PICTURE PERFECT ENTERTAINMENT, INC.,
PICTURE PERFECT FILMS, CAREER WORKS
AND/OR JON RAGIN; ALL FUNDS HELD IN ALL
ACCOUNTS MAINTAINED AT CHASE BANK,
INCLUDING, BUT NOT LIMITED TO ACCOUNT
NUMBER 888005516965, IN THE NAME OF
JON RAGIN; ALL FUNDS HELD IN ANY
ACCOUNT AT FLEET BANK IN THE NAME
OF JON RAGIN; AND ALL PROCEEDS TRACEABLE
TO THE FILM "CRIME PARTNERS", INCLUDING,
BUT NOT LIMITED TO PROCEEDS FROM VIDEO
SALES, DVD SALES, MUSIC SALES, THEATRICAL
PRODUCTIONS, SOUNDTRACKS, AND ANY AND ALL
PRODUCTIONS RELATED TO THE "CRIME PARTNERS"
FILM.

- -X

FILED UNDER SEAL

**AFFIDAVIT IN SUPPORT
OF SEIZURE WARRANT**

FRANCIS MACE, being duly sworn, deposes and says that he is a Special Agent assigned to the United States Department of Treasury, Internal Revenue Service ("IRS"), Criminal Investigations, duly appointed according to law and acting as such.

1. I have been a Special Agent with the IRS since September 1999. During that time, I have participated in numerous investigations. My training, education and experience includes debriefing numerous cooperating witnesses; monitoring wiretapped conversations of individuals involved in narcotics, tax evasion, fraud and money laundering; conducting numerous searches of locations where money laundering, tax evasion, narcotics and fraud

1

records, evidence and proceeds have been found; and conducting surveillance of individuals engaged in such offenses. Through this training and experience, I have become familiar with the manner in which money laundering, narcotics trafficking, fraud and tax evasions are committed, the method of payment and collection of payment in such schemes, and the efforts of persons involved in such activity to avoid detection by law enforcement.

2.   Information contained in this affidavit is either known to me personally, or was related to me by the person indicated.

3.   This declaration is respectfully submitted pursuant to 18 U.S.C. §§ 981(a)(1)(C), 981(b)(3), 1029, 1956 and 1957 and 21 U.S.C. Sections 853, in support of the Government's application for a warrant authorizing the seizure of the above-referenced property. The information contained herein is based on my personal knowledge in conducting a criminal investigation of Kenneth McGriff, Jon Ragin, and others, the records and files of the United States of America and information communicated to me by other law enforcement agents and by reliable confidential sources of information. Because this affidavit is being submitted for a limited purpose, I have not set forth every fact that I have learned over the course of the investigation.

2

ARREST AND SEARCH WARRANTS

3.   On or about January 2, 2003, a complaint was filed under seal in the Eastern District of New York charging defendant Jon Ragin with money laundering and credit card fraud, pursuant to 18 U.S.C. §§ 1029, 1956, 1957. On January 3, 2003, law enforcement agents arrested the defendant Jon Ragin. Further, on January 3, 2003, a search warrant was authorized by the Court and executed at 240 Rutland Road, Brooklyn, New York and 175-20 Wexford Terrace, Apartment 11F, Queens, New York.

4.   Further, on January 2, 2003, the Honorable James C. Francis IV, United States Magistrate Judge for the Southern District of New York, issued a warrant authorizing the search of the Murder, Inc. office, on the basis of the allegations set forth in my affidavit.

5.   In support of this affidavit, I rely on the allegations set forth in the January 2, 2003 affidavit in support of a search warrant of the premises known as Murder, Inc. and the January 2, 2002 affidavit in support of arrest warrant of Jon Ragin and search warrant of Ragin's premises. The allegations contained in those warrants are incorporated by reference in its entirety.

BACKGROUND CONCERNING KENNETH "SUPREME" MCGRIFF

6.   In the early 1980s, Kenneth "Supreme" McGriff founded the "Supreme Team," a notorious street gang which operated in the vicinity of the Baisley Park Houses in Queens, New York.

3

McGriff and the other gang members adhered to the tenets of a quasi- religious sect known as the "Five Percenters." Under McGriff'S leadership, the gang concentrated its criminal efforts on the widespread distribution of crack-cocaine. By 1987, the Supreme Team's drug receipts exceeded $200,000 a day, and the gang regularly committed acts of violence and murder to maintain its stronghold on the area's drug trade. In the late 1980s and early 1990s, following a series of federal prosecutions in the Eastern District of New York, several Supreme Team members were convicted of federal racketeering, including predicate acts of murder, crack-cocaine distribution and other charges. See generally United States v. Miller, 116 F.3d 641 (2d Cir. 1997)(discussing the conviction of Supreme Team members). Among those convicted was McGriff'S nephew and second-in-command, Gerald "Prince" Miller.

7. In 1989, McGriff was convicted in the Eastern District of New York for his participation in a Continuing Criminal Enterprise, and related felony narcotics offenses, in connection with his operation of the Supreme Team. The charges primarily arose from McGriff'S massive crack-cocaine business in the Baisley Housing Projects in Queens, New York. He was sentenced to a term of 12 years incarceration, and completed his sentence in approximately 1995. He is no longer on supervised release in connection with that offense.

8. The investigation has revealed that following

4

McGriff's release from prison, he resumed his criminal activity. In particular, McGriff began transporting narcotics from New York to the Baltimore, Maryland area, among other locations. Thereafter, in an effort to launder his drug money, McGriff helped found the Murder, Inc. record label, utilizing the proceeds from his drug empire.

9. Since McGriff's release from prison, he has obtained various forms of false identification and possessed firearms on multiple occasions. In fact, law enforcement officers have recovered the false identification from his person during two arrests since 2001, and he currently faces both federal and state gun charges.

10. With regard to the state gun charge, in July 2001, NYPD officers stopped McGriff while driving a BMW in Harlem. Thereafter, the officers observed that McGriff was carrying a loaded, .40 caliber pistol in his waistband. Pursuant to search incident to arrest, the officers discovered that McGriff was carrying approximately $10,000 in cash and a New Jersey driver's license bearing his photograph and the name "Lee Tuten." McGriff told the arresting officers that his name was "Rick Coleman" and that he was an "executive" for Def Jam. He was charged in the state with possession of a weapon with intent to use, and was released on bail. On or about September 26, 2002, McGriff pleaded guilty in state court to attempted criminal possession of a weapon

5

with intent to use. He was scheduled to be sentenced for that offense in January 2003 and was permitted to remain out on bail in the interim.

11. In late November 2002, and again in late December 2002, McGriff flew to Texas under the alias "Ricky Coleman," and stayed at the Four Seasons Hotel in Houston under that alias. Hotel and prison records reflect that during both of McGriff'S trips to Texas, he traveled via limousine to Beaumont, where the lieutenant for his drug operation, Gerald "Prince" Miller, currently is incarcerated. Prison officials advise that Miller is being investigated, because guards repeatedly have observed a sharp increase in the presence of heroin in the prison facility, coinciding with McGriff'S visits. Subpoenaed hotel records reflect that for both of McGriff'S trips to Texas, Murder, Inc. paid for McGriff'S hotel stays and incidentals, including the $1,200 limousine rides to the Beaumont prison facility.

12. With respect to the federal gun charge, on or about November 18, 2002, prosecutors in this investigation obtained a sealed indictment against McGriff through the Baltimore U.S. Attorney's Office, charging him with illegal weapons possession by a felon in violation of 18 U.S.C. § 922(g), the basis of which is described in greater detail below. On December 28, 2002, law enforcement officers arrested McGriff at the Loews Hotel in Miami Beach, Florida on the federal gun warrant. Subpoenaed hotel

6

records reflect that McGriff checked into the hotel under the alias "Rick Coleman." Subpoenaed records also show that McGriff paid $1,000 in cash at the outset of the stay and informed hotel representatives to expect payment from Murder, Inc. by the time McGriff checked out, at which time the $1,000 would be returned to McGriff. At the time of the arrest, McGriff was in possession of the Murder, Inc. pager. In addition, McGriff had multiple identifications in the names McGriff and Ricky Coleman, the alias McGriff has used to engage in travel paid for by Murder, Inc. McGriff also used a Murder, Inc. corporate American Express credit card in the name of Christopher Lorenzo,[1] for a recent stay at the Four Seasons Hotel in Houston, Texas.

MURDER, INC.

13. Murder, Inc., which is located on the 29 Floor of 825 8th Avenue, New York, NY, is in the business of developing, producing, promoting and distributing the work of various musical artists, with an emphasis on the rap genre.

14. A review of various public filings reflects that Murder, Inc. was founded in the late 1990s. Presently, the company has a partnership with another record label called "Island Def Jam Music Group" ("Def Jam"), which itself is a subsidiary of a company called Universal Music Group.

15. The CEO of Murder, Inc. is an individual named

---

[1]Brother of Murder, Inc. CEO Irving Lorenzo, AKA "Irv Gotti."

7

Irving Lorenzo, who publicly utilizes the street name "Irv Gotti."
As set forth in greater detail below, Gotti founded Murder, Inc.
with the aid of Kenneth "Supreme" McGriff, a well-known organized
crime boss with a prior federal conviction for engaging in a
Continuing Criminal Enterprise and narcotics trafficking. McGriff
is the titular leader of a notorious gang, the "Supreme Team,"
which over the course of the past two decades has been responsible
for multiple homicides and the sale of vast quantities of heroin,
cocaine and cocaine-base in Queens, New York and elsewhere.
McGriff and Gotti established Murder, Inc., in part, utilizing
proceeds from the McGriff's drug empire.

16. McGriff continues to be involved in illegal
activity, including possession of firearms by a convicted felon,
identification fraud, and extensive narcotics trafficking which
generates substantial proceeds for McGriff and his co-conspirators.
His drug trafficking activities are confirmed by, among other
things, his lengthy history of narcotics-related offenses;
information provided by reliable, confidential informants; text
messages transmitted on a two-way pager paid for by Murder, Inc.;
evidence recovered pursuant to a search warrant from a drug stash
house where McGriff's fingerprints were lifted; and proof linking
McGriff to a narcotics-related, double homicide which occurred
outside the stash house. Moreover, despite evidence that McGriff
has earned substantial income from his illicit activities and

8

position at Murder, Inc., a check of IRS records reflects that for the past six years, McGriff has not filed any tax returns. Neither Murder, Inc. nor any other company has filed any documents declaring McGriff as an employee. Simply put, McGriff has no known legitimate source of income.

17. McGriff has a well-known reputation for violence and witness intimidation. His fame for founding the notorious "Supreme Team" gang is discussed in numerous rap lyrics and news articles. In addition, the investigation has revealed McGriff's involvement in several, highly-publicized shootings and homicides related to narcotics trafficking and the rap industry. Murder, Inc., in turn, exploits McGriff's notoriety for business advantage, by instilling fear in members of the music industry. Toll records confirm that McGriff has transmitted a message over a Murder, Inc., two-way pager bragging that his reputation keeps people "in line" and teaches others "never to fuck with" Murder, Inc. The investigation also has received information regarding Murder, Inc.'s use of McGriff's reputation to extort a prominent music executive from another company.

McGRIFF'S INVOLVEMENT WITH MURDER, INC.

18. McGriff has had, and continues to have, a significant, yet largely secret, position in Murder, Inc. As shown in greater detail below, the investigation has demonstrated that:

19. Murder, Inc. regularly transmits large sums of money

9

to McGriff via payroll and/or invoice checks, which the company issues to McGriff under false identities.

20. Murder, Inc. funds McGriff's frequent air travel and hotel stays throughout the United States using false identifications.

21. Murder, Inc. provides McGriff with a two-way, text-messaging pager, which McGriff uses to communicate with his criminal associates concerning, among other things, narcotics trafficking.

22. McGriff regularly is present at the Murder, Inc. Office on a weekly basis. McGriff is often inside the CEO's office, and knows where the CEO's keys are hidden.

23. McGriff has told law enforcement officers that he is an "executive" at Def Jam, which is in partnership with Murder, Inc.

24. Agents recently surveilled McGriff traveling from a court appearance on a pending New York State gun charge to the building where the Murder, Inc. Office is located. A guard at the building identified McGriff as "Mr. Supreme" who works for Murder, Inc.

25. A compact disk jacket of a Murder, Inc. album lists "Supreme" as "Murder Management."

26. McGriff regularly instructs his criminal associates to call him at the Murder, Inc. Office.

10

27. McGriff is involved in the negotiation and review of business contracts on behalf of Murder, Inc.

28. In connection with Murder, Inc., McGriff is the co-executive producer of a soon-to-be-released film, "Crime Partners." The other two executive producers of the movie, Jon Ragin and Wayne Davis, are long time narcotics traffickers. Davis, like McGriff, has a federal conviction for engaging in a criminal enterprise. Ragin was recently released from lifetime parole for a New York state narcotics trafficking conviction. In addition, Ragin currently operates a large-scale, multi-million dollar credit card fraud ring. Neither Ragin nor McGriff have any legitimate source of income, although Davis reports modest income from a clothing store position. All three are believed to have invested proceeds from their criminal endeavors into the film. During an interview with a magazine, McGriff bragged that he funded the movie with proceeds of crime. Murder, Inc. is actively promoting the film on its website and in other media outlets. In addition, Murder, Inc. is producing the movie soundtrack.

THE "CRIME PARTNERS" FILM

29. Agents have reviewed advertisements for a soon-to-be-released film, "Crime Partners," the trailer of which can be viewed on the Murder, Inc. Records Website. Murder, Inc. is also producing and distributing the movie soundtrack. The film stars Ice-T, Snoop Doggie Dog and other well-known rap artists. The

11

117

website for the distributer of the film, Creative Light, lists McGriff and Jon Ragin as two of the executive producers of the movie. As reported in multiple, recent magazine articles, various journalists have interviewed Ragin and McGriff regarding their involvement with this movie. Moreover, as discussed in greater detail below, McGriff, like Ragin, has a lengthy criminal record involving narcotics trafficking and has no known legitimate source of income. The investigators believe that Ragin and McGriff have laundered proceeds from their criminal activities through the film.

30. Raven Knite Productions is the production company and the registered agent for the film. I am informed by DEA agents that in or about 1999, DEA intercepted a package sent from Ragin to Raven Knite Productions, after a specially trained canine alerted positively to the presence of narcotics inside the package. When the package was opened, it was found to contain approximately $5,000 in cash, wrapped in scented baby wipes. I am aware, based on my training and experience, that narcotics traffickers frequently package their drug proceeds in scented material in an effort to evade law enforcement interception and detection. Advertisements for the film displayed in magazines reflect that another company called Picture Perfect Films[2] is distributing the movie. Analysis of checks drawn on Picture Perfect Films' bank

_____

[2]As discussed in greater detail below, Ragin sometimes refers to himself as "Picture Perfect Dude" when communicating with his criminal associates.

account at Fleet Bank show that Ragin and McGriff's sister, Barbara McGriff, have signatory authority on the account.

31. The Internet Web sites for the distributer of the film, Creative Light, lists McGriff, Jon Ragin and Wayne Davis as the executive producers of the movie. As reported in multiple, recent magazine articles, various journalists have interviewed Ragin, McGriff and Davis regarding their involvement with this movie. All three of the executive producers: (1) have lengthy criminal records involving narcotics trafficking; (2) have either modest income (in the case of Davis), or no known legitimate source of income (in the case of Ragin and McGriff); and (3) are believed to have been involved with laundering proceeds from criminal activities through the film.

32. Jon Ragin, one of the three executive producers, has been the subject of investigation for several years for his participation in narcotics trafficking and credit card fraud. Currently, Ragin is believed to be one of the leaders of a large-scale credit card fraud scheme. He is one of two registered owners of a sham company called "Tuxedo Rental." Bank records reflect that in 1998,[3] Murder, Inc. issued a check in the amount of over $10,000, made out to "Jon Ragin-Tuxedo Rental."

33. McGriff and Ragin are also the close associates of Wayne Davis, the third executive producer of the "Crime Partners"

---

[3]Murder, Inc. did not begin filing any tax returns until 1999.

13

119

film. In 1989, Wayne Davis was convicted after a jury trial in the Southern District of New York of engaging in a Continuing Criminal Enterprise, conspiracy to distribute heroin, and sale of a controlled substance within 1,000 feet of a school, and was sentenced to a term of 20 years imprisonment to be followed by lifetime parole. At one point during the proceedings in that case, a mistrial was declared after investigators uncovered a plot to murder a potential government witness. See United States v. Arrington, et al., 867 F.2d 122 (2d Cir. 1989). Davis was released from prison in or about 1998 and currently is under the supervision of U.S. Probation. The Probation Officer advises that when questioned, Davis denied any involvement in the movie. In 2001, Davis reported modest income (approximately $26,000) from a clothing store position.

34. Further, during the execution of a search warrant at a stash house located in Baltimore, agents discovered several video cassette tapes, which bear a recording date of the year 2000 and appear to be "behind the scenes" recordings made on the set of the film "Crime Partners." As noted above, Murder, Inc. is actively promoting the film, the trailer of which can be viewed on the Murder, Inc. website. Murder, Inc. also is producing and distributing the movie soundtrack. McGriff can be seen on the videotape stuffing what appear to be large amounts of cash down his pants.

14

McGRIFF'S INVOLVEMENT IN NARCOTICS AND HOMICIDES

35. The investigation has shown McGriff's involvement in homicides and a shooting. These acts of violence have been linked to both narcotics trafficking and the rap music industry. In one instance, McGriff directed co-conspirators to kill an drug associate who, agents believe, McGriff suspected of cooperating with the government. In another instance, McGriff was involved with the shooting of another rap artist named "50 Cent" who wrote a song exposing McGriff'S criminal activities. Confirmation of McGriff'S violent activities are demonstrated by reliable, confidential informants; toll analysis of the Murder, Inc. Pager; and evidence obtained via search warrants at a narcotics stash house where McGriff's fingerprints were recovered.

36. The defendant Jon Ragin has a long history of involvement of trafficking in narcotics and counterfeit credit cards. Ragin has no known legitimate source of income, and is on lifetime parole for a New York State cocaine conviction. A check of records maintained by the IRS reflects that for the past six years, Ragin has not filed any tax returns. No company has filed any documents with the IRS declaring Ragin as an employee.

37. As shown in greater detail below, the investigation has shown that Ragin and his associates are conducting a large-scale credit card fraud scheme which operates as follows. First, Ragin and his associates steal valid credit card account numbers.

15

121

"I've been patiently waiting
For a track to explode on
You get stunned if you want
And yo ass'll get rolled on
A fuse like my flows
Been hot for so long
If you thinkin I'ma fuckin
Fall of your so wrong"

—*50 Cent, "Patiently Waiting", 2003*

Chapter 9
Patiently Waiting:
50, Eminem, and Dr. Dre

Dr. Dre is the Crystal of rap, the elite, the name brand you know you can trust. Hip Hop's Hoover Vacuum, the preferred consumer choice among suburban households, sucking up all of the hottest talent hip hop has had to offer over the past 20 years. Add Eminem into the deal and you have the equivalent of the Guarantee on the box, that 100% Satisfaction-Guaranteed sticker that reinforces the confidence in the teenager spending their week's allowance on a record that he or she is sure to be another satisfied customer.

Since Dre signed Eminem in 1998 to his Aftermath Entertainment label, the two have created a hip-hop monopoly, but it wasn't until they collectively signed 50 Cent that Aftermath became a cottage industry. Dre had done it once before with Death Row Records in the early 1990s, but the 50 Cent signing was the millennium's equivalent of Suge Knight signing Tupac Shakur, only this time it was Dre who was cleaning up.

It was his time now, but the stars had also lined up for Eminem, who had brought 50 Cent to Dre's attention and co-signed him to Shade Records, as well as for 50 himself, who was experiencing a rebirth of sorts after almost watching his career chances flatline with him literally after a now-legendary near-fatal shooting in 2000. While 50 was recouping and rebuilding his strength and arsenal (both lyrically and as a hustler), Dre and Em laying their own groundwork for the greatness that would follow for all—constructing the foundation for what would become hip hop's first Roman Empire.

The Legislature for this hip-hop empire would be composed of a number of key figures who worked instrumentally behind the scenes to help Em and Dre stage rap's biggest coup since Death Row's, and in truth, it was a comeback for everyone involved. Jimmy Iovine and Ted Field, the co-owner/operators of Interscope Records had been on the verge of bankruptcy in 1991 when they hooked up with Dre and Suge and signed on as Death Row's distributor.

While they had managed as a label throughout the later 1990s after Death Row's commercial demise, they had not caught lightning in a bottle since with any single artist, let along phenomenon, until Eminem came along. Even when they signed Dre as a solo artist in 1995 and gave him his own $10 million label deal, they were prospecting. Dre's debut release on Aftermath, a compilation, along with his follow-up, The Firm, both flopped commercially, but Interscope was quietly happy to take the loss because they knew Dre's track record was highlighted not only by his oil gushers when they hit, but also his instinctive ability to mine for hits as well.

This instinct was evinced namely by his preference for working with up and coming artists, where Dre could smell the money even before the next iconic emcee started flowing, let alone the cash stream that typically followed thereafter. Ready examples include Ice Cube, Snoop Dogg, DOC, and of course Eminem. While Interscope had not yet hit solid gold with the Doctor by 1998, knowing Dre's creative karma, Jimmy Iovine knew it was only a matter of time before the next big claim came along, and sure enough, Eminem was the next big Gusher.

Little did anyone know that Eminem was a mogul in the making, with ambitions of his own beyond emceeing, and with Dre and Interscope, he had the perfect from which to learn—and a quick study he was. Talent has always gravitated toward Dre, but with Em as hip hop's new rainmaker, he had an ear to the street that was exclusive to his own generation of rising emcees, all admiring and aspiring to achieve even a slice of what Eminem had in his meteoric takeover of hip hop in the late 1990s and early years of the millennium.

In the case of 50 Cent, who had already technically been given his first shot, he had ended up receiving 9 more that sidelined him, giving him time to evaluate the kind of shot he had left at greatness. His deal with Jam Master Jay's Columbia Records-distributed label was B-rate when considering the top-shelf brand that Aftermath Entertainment had to offer, in terms both of exposure, muscle, hustle, and credibility.

50 knew he would need all of the above to stage the kind of comeback that would erase his past, and pave a future for him that would guarantee the kind of greatness his talent commanded. As 50 himself explained, the only way the latter was 100% guaranteed in terms of the opportunity was to sign with an organization that was already number 1, and could provide him the proper support to make his rise.

Given 50's experience with his previous label, Columbia Records, he took his time deciding. Once word got out about Eminem's interest, a bidding war broke out, wherein other labels were offering him bigger advances than even the deal with Dre and Em was. In 50's eyes however, advances were short money, and from 50's vantage point, the real money was coming on the backend, and so he invested his faith as such.

Additionally, while the media would spin the 'Eminem discovered 50' angle in introducing the rapper to the public, the reality was that 50 had been around for years and it was in fact both rappers' attorneys who had turned one onto the other, as opposed to Eminem discovering 50 rapping on a street corner. The public presentation of 50's 'discovery' by rap's hottest commodity, Em, was key to establishing him as a legitimate 'protégé, wherein rap fans would embrace 50 no-questions-asked, giving him the instant credibility and therein sales that they had Eminem back in 1999 when Dre 'put Em on.'

Rap fans had bought into Eminem so quickly because of his talent no doubt, but what put him over the top was the 'Dre protégé' sticker, which gave the white rapper a stamp of endorsement in the credibility department that would have otherwise taken years to earn. Fans wanted to believe that Dre had magically discovered Eminem's demo, but in reality, while the 'Dre discovered Em' twist was spun by Interscope publicists, it was Interscope CEO Jimmy Iovine who had first suggested to Dre that he take Eminem on as an artist, knowing the rapper's affiliation with Aftermath would go farther in cementing his authenticity to hip hop fans than if he had been merely introduced through Interscope, who were viewed as a corporate, mainstream conglomerate.

The same strategy was at work with 50's signing, wherein a heavy, corporate machinery at work behind the curtains, the signing of 50 was a team effort, and Em and Dre were happy to play along where they had to, as they all stood to make a fortune. Eminem's label, Shade Records, was distributed through Aftermath, and thereafter through Interscope, such that Eminem owned a quarter stake in 50's contract, Dre a quarter, and Interscope the other half.

No matter the numbers, to the hip hop public, it was ultimately Eminem's visible fascination with 50's unique delivery and style, coupled with the anticipation of Dre's production, that got the buzz circulating on the street about 50 as fast as it did. As 50 explained the entire deal's unfolding, "Theo, my attorney, and Paul Rosenberg, Eminem's attorney and management, work closely together—they grew up and kind of came up together. And I gave them a CD I put out called Guess Who's Back and Em was in the middle of finishing The Eminem Show, and when he was done he got a chance to listen to it and at the time he was saying that he was kind of bored with what was going on with the same crews, the same artists, and that he wanted to do something different."

"When he had the opportunity to listen to it, he was like, 'Yo, this is it right here.' So, when he heard it, he was excited. So he took it to Dre, and they had me fly out. He called me on a Friday at 9 o'clock at night and was like, 'Yo, we need you to come out and meet with us tomorrow. What was weird was, like, I got the call on Friday at 9 o'clock at night and they wanted me to fly out the next day. I had other offers on the table from other companies like Universal, J Records, Jive Records, Warner Bros., Capitol, a few other companies—you know, those situations take place from 9 to 5 and Monday through Friday, like during your working hours."

"It felt a little different, so I flew out met with them the following day in an editing studio, and Dre stopped by and we kicked it, and when I left, I knew I was doing the deal with them, which ended up being for a $1 million advance. So I got back to the city, and then the offers skyrocketed: The offers were all the way up to a $1.6 million once the companies realized that Dr. Dre and Eminem were interested."

"I wasn't that excited with the initial phone call because I had (been to) so many meetings before that it really wasn't (fun). The creative part is my pleasure, the fun part for me. With business, you have to be able to separate the (artistry). Some artists are so into the (art form), they might as well be painters with a smock and French accent because they're going to get ripped off. Some people's talent is to write music or sing, or rap and other people's talent is to take advantage of those people. The numbers just went crazy. But when I had left (the meeting with Em and Dre), I had made this decision that I wanted to be on Shady/Aftermath, before I left just cuz the idea of being signed to them, of not having anyone trying to censor me, was a great idea."

"For everything else that comes with being successful as an artist. The notoriety—for people to recognize your talent. At the end of the day I felt like just sayin' Eminem's sales weren't strugglin' Dr Dre's sales weren't strugglin' and I felt like it was because they were putting together the type of projects that have been really quality projects! It was cool, I did the deal for like, a million dollars, but I still gained so much more out of working with Eminem and Dr. Dre that the other change for me means nothing. I'm in a good space right now."

While 50 may have been in a good place, the industry itself was not, rather in desperate need of a sales boost. 2002 was the weakest year in sales for hip hop of the past 5. The only major label recording artist who did was Eminem, 50's label boss, and once word of the signing got out, everyone's hopes shot through the roof, along with the odds that 50 would meet and exceed those expectations. No one was more excited than Eminem himself about 50's prospects for greatness, "I kept hearing things (about 50), then my manager hit me off with a CD."

"I had been in a slump, thinking 'Where's hip hop gonna go? When I heard 50's stuff, it was like 'Ok, let's see who 50's talking to now? Let's see what the story is on him?'... (Now with his album), I'm there doing the mix downs and me and Dre are just overseeing the whole project, making sure that every song is hot...I wish my first album was this hot. That's all I can say. I'm not selling the album. The album is going to sell itself." Dre echoed Em's sentiments on 50's promise as the next great step in hip hop's evolution artistically and commercially, "50 came out here to L.A. for a couple of days and he seemed like he was cool as shit. 50 is one of the most incredible artists I worked with as far as writing, basic performance and vibing. He came in, and every track I put up, he had something for it. He wrote to it. He got in the booth and did his thing. 50's album in my opinion is gonna compete with all the classic hip-hop LP's that came out in the last 10 years. It's right up there. Shit came out hot." As rappers, the respect between the Eminem and 50 seemed authentically mutual, as 50 explained, ""I'm almost the hottest rapper…I signed a deal with the hottest rapper. Eminem is so talented, it's annoying—he got a gift."

"If you believe in God, you believe in fate, and I think he's exactly what God intended him to be. You can look at him and see what he's doing on television and he's doing whatever shit he's doing and however the script should be or however the video director chose the set is what you see, but when you kick it with him and you kind of get to know him and you work alongside him, he's not even into this shit."

"He's into music, he just wants to make music. And the success that comes with it, your head might be so big—I know I'd be running around, you'd all probably have to tap me on the shoulder to turn my head because it's so big, my hat won't fit. But he's the biggest artist you there right now, and from my experience, from what I see from being around him, he gets more enjoyment out of making the music than he does out of seeing what it actually does in numbers after he's done with it. I think Eminem is the best period. The best. I'm starting to figure it out. I think that what happened to Em happened so fast that he hasn't even really realized how big he is. He's still down-to-earth and humble, despite the fact that he can rap circles around the game. He's so talented sometimes it can become annoying. Plus he can't really toot his own horn, it makes people uneasy; but I can. The boy is No. 1.

We're alike in a lot of ways, he speaks a lot from his life experience, otherwise you wouldn't know who Kim was. I do the same, it's just a little more gunplay, more life-threatening situations…"

"He may not be my favorite person to listen to all the time, but he does rap about his real life issues. If not you wouldn't know how he feels about his mother, who Hailey is, who Kim is. Those situations—he's using his real life situations (in his raps), and that's what I do. You see what I'm sayin'? So I respect it when I listen to it. I enjoy it cuz it's really what's going on with him and how he feels, he's expressing it through his music. I do the same thing. So I look at and go 'He's one of the best to me like when I listen to him.' And then I get to work beside him so I know how much he puts into how his music comes out. He's a perfectionist, he (and) Dre (are) really perfectionists."

Once all the contracts were signed and advances disbursed, 50 went into the studio to begin work on what would become the biggest selling hip hop album of 2003. For 50, the creative process moved along as seamlessly as his signing with Em and Dre had, wherein the environment was one in which "it exceeded my expectations. It's more that I ever thought it would be. It's almost to the point where we're not working. It's that easy. Everyone knows exactly what they're supposed to do and they're executing (it). Shit just got done so fast. I had 48 records recorded prior to the deal being done. They took 16 records of the 48 that they felt like had to stay…I got a lot of extra music so I can use them on soundtracks and other placements…I got the best rappers, best producers around me…Its' the best music that I've recorded to date, I've got the best production—Dr. Dre, Eminem, Roc Wilder Twee Lo, Diggah…I'm getting better! This is like my album will be twice as good as my last album."

"Where I'm at right now I don't even see anybody. My competition is just to fit in with Eminem and Dre…My album is so well put together. Eminem says he wishes his first album was like mine.

(Instead of) comparing it to classics like, Illmatic or Reasonable Doubt, he said that this album sounds like an album that's made after you know exactly what you're doing...I'm not even trying to keep up with anyone else in the music business outside of Em and Dre."

On another level entirely, 50 definitely felt confident in the aftermath of signing with Dre and Em that he had made the right career decision, "One thing I know for sure is that I'm content with myself. I see the expectations that people have around me already since I signed the deal (with Shady Records). It makes no difference to me when people sit around and wishing for me to do bad, I'm already doing better than people around me would expect. I'm already on cloud 9, I'm floating."

Things moved fast for 50 once he signed the deal, such that "I started right after we signed. They tripped on me because I sent 12 at a time. I didn't want them to listen to so much at once that they couldn't pick what they liked, so I sent 12 at a time. After they listened to (those) records, they decided we're going to do a few more records and that's it. I went to Los Angeles. I was there for five days. I recorded seven records with Dre and then I went to Detroit and did six more records with Em. Four records went on the 8 Mile Soundtrack but we've done some more records since then."

Ultimately, 50's goal in the course of recording his debut album under the deal seemed to be to stay on a competitive level with his mentors, providing him with a constant motivation to give only his best, "I fear not fitting in with Eminem and Dr. Dre. That's what counts to me. The other stuff (the threat of violence) has already been a part of my life, none of that is new. They signed me, so I'll never be equivalent to Eminem or Dr. Dre. If Em says 'I'm the future of music', then what he's saying is he's the future of music because he signed me."

Finally, 50 also seemed to take the notion that he could become hip hop's next overnight icon as seriously from a business point of view as his backers were, wherein he was conscious of the fact that he had been handed a one in a million shot that he couldn't afford to blow, "(Interscope CEO) Jimmy Iovine will tell me, 'I hope you're smart like Dre.' Dre will pull me to the side and tell me to stay focused. I told him in the beginning that my intentions weren't to be trouble. Nobody wants to buy a problem. And with my background, there's a possibility that they'd be purchasing the biggest problem that they've ever found. But because they believed me when I told them I wanted to make music, we were able to progress."

With all the elements brewing properly, the chemistry between 50 as the artist and 50 the commodity were blending according to formula, and with the proper support network in place, the most potent and sometimes unpredictable part of that recipe for greatness, the creation of hit records, was also going off without a hitch.

For 50, in terms of working with the Godfather of hip hop production, the rapper was in creative heaven as an artist, coupled with the fact that there was nothing contrived about the experience from an A&R perspective, leaving 50 free to be himself in the studio and in the context of art-imitating-life. The latter, as much as 50 was watching himself outside of the studio to make sure he stayed clear of trouble, was still an important element to his undeniable authenticity as a rapper, such that it needed to be credibly translated in the lab, "Production-wise, I don't think there's a producer better than Dr. Dre, especially for me."

"He's from NWA—that's like the original gangsta rap group. How he not going to understand my lyrical content? When it gets a little edgy, he gets excited. He's not going, 'Yo, I don't know if you should say that.' He's not calling me in going, 'I think we should switch this line.' I ain't have no boundaries. Em never says 'Don't say that' or 'Can you change that?' If anything, they are always saying that to him. And Dre, he's got to understand what I'm doing, he's from NWA. When I was on Columbia and I dropped 'How To Rob," they actually told me not to cut my hair."

"They thought I was supposed to look like Ol' Dirty Bastard. Just dirty, like, 'You crazy, like the guy who said they would rob everybody.' I couldn't even get it. Like Ol' Dirty Bastard did this record, like how are they supposed to know who I am when I shoot 'Thug Love,' which is the real single for this record? What is it going to look like? What are we going to do? We going to do Trading Places? 'Hey, Mortimer!' Like somebody going to throw some money on the floor and I'm going to change into the new kid? It was just a record, and they wanted to make that the theme with me as an artist, period."

"I'm not with that. Columbia, I don't think that they understood me, period... Dr. Dre and Eminem, they made the final executive decision. I told them what I wanted and we kinda shifted through them. I recorded 12 w/ Dre and I only put 4 on the album so I got plenty of records...With Dre its like, I do vocals, I write the vocals and then Dre would come and we'd do vocals, like we change, not too much, but if he feels like I could say something a lil differently, we'll change that. Dre, he'll play dope beats—they're automatic, (He'll say), 'These are the hits, 50. So pick one of these and make a couple of singles or something.'"

"The very first time he heard (me rap on) 'In Da Club' he said, 'Yo, I didn't think you was going to go there with it, but, you know, it works.' He was probably thinking of going in a different direction with that song. Then he expanded it into a hit record. (Dre and Em) made me a lot better, fast...Creatively, it's a better space for me." For 50, the trust he felt artistically with both Dre and Eminem seemed equally as important as the freedom they gave him there, which 50 qualified by explaining that he felt that trust as implicitly as he did because all three artists were on the same level, "I think Shady/Aftermath is way better than Columbia...re understands being from NWA, my lyrical content."

"And Eminem, picture him saying 'Yo you can't say that.' He's as edgy as you get on his level, so he understands exactly what it is and I think that's what drew him to me—you know when he heard the music. He know what it is, so it's cool. I'm real comfortable (because of that), the work process is—I'll go do it and they'll listen and then they'll say 'Yo, you know what I think you should do, something like this,' and I'll take their advice and pass the world of respect. Cause I know that for sure they are really in my best interest. They are my corner for real. If they didn't come get me to do the deal, what would I be doin?"

The unsettling subtext of the latter question lies in the sobering look it provides into the hustler psychology that truly authentic street rappers live by, wherein, as 50 explained, "I ain't got no Plan B. I ain't never had no job before. My plan wasn't working. I've never even had working papers before. So it was either this or hustling. So I had to do my thing."

Eminem, in addition to being 50's label boss, was so excited about the opportunity to work with a rapper of 50's talent, that the great white hope threw his own hat into the ring as a producer on several of the tracks. 50 had no problem with this because he seemed to be genuinely impressed with Eminem's skills as a producer, such that "Em is so talented it becomes annoying...Every time we go to the studio, he's got something new to play and it's like, 'Oh man, I gotta have something new to play, too.' Em is the rapper's rapper. He listens to everything. Every word, every slang, if you change something he's going to hear it all, (and that comes out in his producing.)" In describing the process of working with Em as a producer, 50 explained, "Em, he spins records and like he send me a skeleton and I'll write to it. Then we'll build the song around it...He usually likes to watch me do what I'm doing. He lets me just do what I want. You know what he'll do? He'll send a skeleton—like the track won't be finished when I get it. I'll rap to a beat that's not even 50 percent done and I'll put the concept down. And then he'll build the record around what I did..."

"At the end of the day, it's not until he actually mixes the record that you'll hear what it is for real. And I've been happy with everything that we've done so far. He mixed a lot of records on this album. He produced and mixed his two records and then he mixed, I think, about five or six other records on the album. He can expand the record. He can make it something that, if someone else has already produced the base of it, he can put what it takes to make it go over the top."

As Eminem explained from a production angle, working with 50 is a dream because "there's not much fixing involved, which is a beautiful thing." In the course of 50's experience collaborating creatively with Dr. Dre and Eminem, the rapper was clearly a student, explaining that, through serious study, trial and error, the duo's magic is "starting to rub off cuz I start to make sure before I send them a record, (its up to their standards.) Cause (before) I would do a record and send it to them to see what they think, and now I kinda put it together better because—(fore example), after Dre records vocals with you, you pick up things from him, cause he's the best producer I've ever worked with."

"And when you record with someone and they change your process, it means you learn something in that situation, so now when I go in the booth and record records on my own, (I got it down.) They could be in LA, Em could be in Detroit and I'm working on a record here, I kind of record it how I think Dre would do it, you see what I'm sayin'? So I know that I'm pickin up new things from being around them, and they should expect my music to be even better."

Once word of 50's signing got out on the street, fans were instantly hungry for anything they could get their hands on in the way of material from the rapper, and while New York fans had the benefit of the mix tape market, where 50 had made his underground come up, the suburban hip hop fans, which constitute roughly 60% of the consumer market for the genre, would soon get their fix. In perfect timing, Eminem's signing of 50 Cent coincided with the upcoming release of the rapper's debut film, '8 Mile', the soundtrack of which was being released on Shade Records.

A sure-fire hit with fans, Dre, Em and Interscope made sure the soundtrack was 50 cent heavy on material, knowing they could not have asked for a more ideal vehicle by which to introduce 50 Cent to the public in lieu of the release of his debut LP. 50's breakout hit from the soundtrack was 'Wanksta', which the rapper himself explained as "my joint, right there. That's the first one that broke for me off the 8 mile joint. I'm happy with that, like for me and sales on the soundtrack. It took off by itself, we was gonna do 'Places To Go' at first and then the record. We started on the mixtape with it and then Funkmaster Flex got it and he liked the record and they just went crazy on it. You know? So it worked out for me I'm blessed with that."

Elaborating on the process for choosing which songs would be included on '8 Mile' to introduce 50, the rapper reveals that he played an integral role in choosing the tracks, but also points out that the whole process was inspired, such that greatness was hanging overhead the whole time, "'Me I Call The Shots Round Here', that was off the '8 Mile' Soundtrack too. Actually, Rakim wrote to that record and I did it over you know?…That's a Dre joint and I took the beat, cause that's what I do—I take the beat. I did it over cause I thought the beat was hot and I put my own song together on it. (But its crazy that it was Rakim's first)." The core of '8 Mile' focuses on the street art of battle rapping, knowing in the hip hop underground as 'battling', the premier way to make a name for oneself as an emcee on the street level, and the vehicle by which Eminem first came up in Detroit's hip hop underground.

While this type of contest is also popular in New York and around the country, as it has been for years prior to the release of '8 Mile', 50 Cent, ironically, never made his name this way, preferring the mixtape route for one bottom line reason, there was money involved. As he explains, in true hustler fashion, "No, I never battled. You know why? Because I never (saw)any money in battling. To be honest with you, I'm from the bottom. The music business is a business where no (prerequisites) are necessary. Eminem is a drop out, I'm a drop out, and we both making more money than our high school teachers do."

With 50 and Eminem linked at the hip in the media, rap pundits and critics naturally sought to compare the two, a tendency that 50 saw as natural when the player-hater factor was considered, such that "more people hate Eminem than 50 Cent because Eminem is number one...It's just a different class of people that hate Eminem (than hate me). People that hate Eminem get a headache every time they see his face because he's so good."

"You got actors out there that still don't have films that break $100 million, but Eminem (did that on his) first go around." For 50 Cent, the bottom line in terms of the media comparisons between him and Em was that it gave 50 that much more to live up to creatively and commercially on an overall level with critics, fans, and executives, while personally, setting a certain bar for himself to achieve what his mentors had on all relevant levels.

50 clearly had the confidence as an artist, due in large part to the support system he had at work for him behind the scenes. Within his personal life, 50's most immediate personal life change seemed to be his most desired when he had first signed with Em and Dre, that being "I ain't gotta worry about bills...Finances changed a lot." The fringe benefit of groupie love also suited the rapper just fine, such that "I feel like I got a facelift...The ho's they treat me so much better...I'm eligible (now) for a whole lot of women that I'm not eligible for. They found that them checks get cut, things get different. Like I look better or something, they treat me better."

Aware of the role his overnight celebrity had played in securing the additional trim, 50 seemed to be receiving the attention from the right perspective, such that "you just take it in stride. Yeah, it's fun…I mean as long as you know why the situation is happening, you be alright." Perhaps hip hop's most resilient new emcee, 50 Cent's signing with Shady/Aftermath would go onto revitalize hip hop's sales slump with the 2003 release of 'Get Rich or Die Trying', and most importantly, inject the reality back into rap. 50 was already on top of the world, on his way into the outer space of stardom. What many hip hop fans didn't know was that he'd spent years getting there, and had gotten his start from another hip hop legend…

Chapter 10
Get Rich or Die Trying

The release of 'Get Rich or Die Trying' was 50 Cent's second commercial wind, but probably also his last real chance at a shot for the title at hip hop greatness. This statement might sound overdramatic to those unaware of the pressures facing 50 in his personal life, problems that only success in his professional life could solve. While he presented the crack trade as an alternative means by which to support his family in the absence of success as a rap star, in reality this was not a viable long term means to sustain his welfare, let alone that of his family.

50 knew this, but likely felt uneasy about revealing this fact that his fans, aware that it might serve to weaken his hardened hustler exterior. Only Tupac had been able to have a completely open dialogue with his fans in this vein, successfully discussing his internal contradictions and insecurities on record with listeners. This was because Shakur spoke through his music for such a broad, diverse demographic—that being the inherent insecurities of the African American community at large.

Hustler vs. human being, player vs. father, and so forth. Because Tupac was the first to admit to his own downfalls and failures amid his successes, the sweeping generalizations he made on behalf of his community's own shortcomings were embraced and accepted, often celebrated because they were painted in a light that pointed light on them often without pointing any individual blame.

Society shouldered alot of the blame, and Tupac succeeded in conceptualizing the failures of the African American community in a way that made acceptable excuses and justifications for why those weaknesses existed and were consistently prevalent in his community. For example, yes, young Black Males sold crack cocaine, which contributed to creating a deadly and irreparable epidemic of addiction and crime in the inner cities. However, they had no other viable alternatives by which to feed their families because society had written off the black community generations ago, and had designed an economic system by which to keep African Americans permanently an underclass.

This contention was supported by thousands of pages of statistics collected by the US Government, who according to Tupac also we partially responsible for creating those statistics. Tupac had informed enough of a mind to see this grand scheme for what it was, including all players and their respective roles and responsibilities in creating and continuing it, both black and white, and verbally was able to assign blame in ways that couldn't really be disputed by either side, namely because Tupac took his share of the responsibility for his actions, and those of his community on their behalf where they were wrong, but also held society to account for its part in creating the conditions in which those actions were inevitable.

Tupac, like an older brother, took the heat and laid the foundation for future generations of rappers to speak more honestly, freely, and most importantly, personally, on the affects their community's up and downsides had on them as people amid being emcees, and created a special place for their contradictions as humans to exist comfortably within that hustler identity.

Tupac had humanized hip hop, allowing rappers to be seen as people, and not just as stars, and therein making it easy for listeners to relate to their own psychologically and socially, realizing their commonality within the black community at large. Shakur was largely responsible for creating an environment where that awareness could exist in general. Ultimately, Tupac was hip hop's seminal martyr, and he made the ultimate sacrifice for his race, artistic peers and fans by symbolizing all their inherent fears, glory, sadness, insecurities, contradictions, strengths, weaknesses, resilience, brilliance, and naivety in one time.

50 Cent was forced to answer the calls of comparison between himself and the late Shakur as his album release approached, pointing out that he was not a role model, rather a reflection of the realities of the inner city, just as Tupac had been, "When I wrote my record I wasn't writing it to be a role model. The music on Get Rich or Die Tryin' is a direct reflection of the environment I come from. Some places they don't understand it because they're not going through the same experiences...

With some artists, people look at them and wanna be that artist. I don't think people wanna be me. I do have defects of character...I don't think it makes me a role model. I think it makes me inspiring. Cos I'm from the bottom I think they look at me and go 'Well, if he made it, I can make it'. Now me myself, I'm not particularly considering myself a role model cause I'm not sensitive, I give people things exactly the way they are, and if they're ready to absorb it they will, and if they aren't they won't."

As 50's album release date neared and 50 was being touted by some critics as the next 'Tupac', it was principally in terms of the potential he had to influence his generation of listeners in equally as powerfully, potent and permanent ways. For 50's own part, he was quick to deflect any notion that he would ever equal Tupac's position or influence over hip hop culture historically and as a whole, because it was irreplaceable, still he did acknowledge that "I've had people say I've saved hip-hop. (But) I think it's a contribution to where we're going next." He went onto clarify that he did desire to be an inspiration as an emcee, in the spirit of Tupac, where he could be, "to me, speaking exactly about my experience is going to encourage other artists to write their experiences."

As a rap icon in-the-making, 50 definitely embodied the promise and potential to be hip hop's next people's champion. He seemed, however, more immediately concerned about ensuring that his deal with Shady/ Aftermath/Interscope was solid, and that he would not be fucked around as he had with Columbia.

Though 50 was cloaked in a sort of underground celebrity already, he was far from out of the woods in terms of every-day worries. In fact, he had more in common with his fellow hustlers than even Tupac had in an everyday sense of things, namely in that 50 had a young child to support, where Tupac died without any offspring. This is perhaps among the only identifiable differences between the two rappers on the surface, barring a measurement in timing and degree within their respective comparisons and similarities—for example, 50 Cent had served prison time prior to becoming a star, where Tupac served his prison time amid his stardom.

Both men had grown up in poverty, perhaps Tupac to a greater degree of severity, having lived in homeless shelters and with a mother who had a severe crack addiction. Still, in an equal degree of tragedy or adversity, 50 Cent had been raised without a mother at all. Both men had had serious attempts on their lives that to date remain unsolved, and the industry drew ready comparisons between the similarity in their rapping delivery style. The greatest parallel between the two men seemed to be their common potential to reach and affect an equal number of listeners, almost to where 50 was picking up the torch where Tupac had left it burning in the blaze of glory and tragedy he left this world amidst.

50 definitely reflected an awareness that he was charged with revitalizing and re-energizing hip hop overall, a sensibility he identified namely by the buzz that excitedly surrounded the release of his music on a national level. Ironically, or perhaps not due to the amount of hip hop music, style and culture that has originated

Coastally in hip hop history, 50 explained that "the anticipation comes from New York. They've been listening to me for two years now, and it's been consistent, good performances. Now their imagination is saying 'I wonder what he'll sound like with Dre and Eminem', being that they are the best producers and rappers in the game." 50 explained the national translation of his local popularity due to positive word-of-mouth regarding the quality of his raps, drawing a direct parallel between street buzz and mainstream retail sales based on his belief that "consistency is the key to all success."

"If I can consistently deliver a good performance, then they won't have to wait until they see a bootlegger and buy it for $5, they'll give up that $16...I believe people need to go to the next level musically. I think the reason why (some people) don't sell is because of the quality of their music...I know the war is going to change things, the economy will change, but quality music still sells. (Consumers) are making a choice to purchase Eminem (for example) instead of some other albums and its obvious by the 8 Mile Soundtrack sales. Other albums are out and they can't even compete and it's not even an album, it's a soundtrack."

In responding to those who quickly pointed to the potentially negative influence 50 could have on the suburban masses based on the inherently negative subject matter within his raps, he argued that this was no more than a reflection of his surroundings, pointing out that this was not his personal preference in reality for his listeners, his own children, or himself, and explaining within that context that "I don't encourage people to do the wrong thing, because the entire time I looked forward to not having to do the wrong thing any more. When I was hustling, I was hustling to try and find enough finances to make legitimate investments."

Still, 50 acknowledged that it would be hard to ever fully shake that past in the general context of his image, in spite of the massive success that would follow, "your last relationship—you're leaving with the luggage. My past is my shadow. Wherever I go, it's going to go with me. I've accepted it. I know no matter what I do I'm going to have an aura around me that isn't really nice. No matter how successful I am or what happens, I don't think I'll shake it."

Still, in spite of his pessimism over ever being allowed to fully outgrow his gangsta image, he fully endorsed the notion of trying to his fans, "like everyone else, you have a past, a history, and people. They say in AA (Alcoholics Anonymous) to kick your habits you gotta change your people, places and things. I'm learnin, I'm growin, I mean everybody as a person should be."

Surprisingly, perhaps most so to his critics, while 50 rapped readily about the good life in his songs, including consuming lots of Crystal Champagne, and on a different level, rapped candidly and specifically about his past selling narcotics, he neither did drugs or drank much at all, explaining that "it doesn't bother me to be around people who smoke weed, but I don't do it. I've been drunk only twice in my life—from champagne. That shit sneaks up on you!"

"Those two times are what kept me away from it. I grew up in a house where my uncles and aunts, they had (substance abuse) problems. They'd get drunk-drunk. One time my uncle got drunk, and these old-timers said, 'I bet you can't move that block of ice from there to there.' He took the bet, picked up the ice, moved it. But it was dry ice. Burned the skin off his fucking hands."

While he didn't do drugs, 50 readily endorsed their sale, especially marijuana, and largely did so because of the naivety of the Government's policy toward preventing the sales of illegal narcotics, reasoning that "they shouldn't legalize drugs. That won't work here. Weed is the hustler's drug to sell. You can have five pounds before it's a felony. A one pound bag is still just a misdemeanor. Let them change the laws for weed to the same laws for cocaine, and people won't smoke that shit no more."

The wisdom in 50's logic on the aforementioned topic came directly as a result of years spent in the streets, witnessing first-hand the neglect of the US Government toward the institutional poverty within the inner city. He seemed to clearly feel that blame for the drug epidemic rested squarely on the shoulders of society at large, not on its specific dealers and users, and as a result, unapologetically endorsed a doctrine of achieving ends by any means—whether they be via hip hop or hustling.

Elaborating on the latter, as 50's career started to take off with the hype surrounding the release of the smash singles 'Wanksta' and then 'In Da Club', the rapper preached a general hustler-edict of money making, dispensing advice to his fans to "concentrate on your money man, try to hold your paper. It takes money to make money so save your money, opportunities come. If you don't have finances to jump on them or at least room to support yourself while you're tryin to move into new situations, then you can't even evolve."

"Like you may see someone in your neighborhood that makes music or do whatever else, and I would say to the hood—get into the music business! This is the business that you have absolutely no requirements, you listen to music, (that's it.) You need no college degree." He explained that the title of his album was a celebration of the pursuit of a better life at any cost, and one that most anyone in a position of adversity could appreciate and relate to, "It's universal. It's the hustle. When you say it with the aura that's around me, it feels negative—get rich or die trying. But if a working class person tells you they're gonna get rich or they're gonna die trying, it just means they're determined."

In seeking to set an example for his fellow hustlers that legal means are as achievable as illicit ones, 50 was setting out to "do something where I'm absolutely unforgettable in business. Trust me. I'm hustling. If Bill Gates'll talk to me long enough, he'll see things my way." Still, while 50 appeared to be endorsing hustling transparently, which is to say regardless of the means toward those ends, he wasn't telling his young listeners to make a career out of drug dealing. Rather, he seemed to be suggesting that if that was their only immediate option, utilize it as they had to toward something more positive, i.e. legitimate, as 50 felt he was doing through his pursuit of hip hop stardom, "don't expect me to evolve into a new person in eight months. People shot me."

"Where I grew up, you were selling drugs or you were starving. Even the people who had jobs came home and sold drugs. My goals are to become something good. It's something positive that I'm supposed to do. I want to move into that space without losing the interest of the people who identify with me. The negative things I say about what I went through, people love that music because it's the theme song to their lives right now. You don't want to lose them. But when I die I want to be remembered as a good person."

Still, in the end of day, even 50 knew the most basic rule to successful self-promotion, that any press is good press. By that rationale, he did little beyond explanation in his raps and in response to direct questions from journalists to combat the image that he was being marketed via, be it negative or positive, as far as how it reflected on 50 as a person. He was principally concerned with how it reflected on him as an emcee and, by extension, on his potential album sales, "I don't care whether (my publicity) is good or bad, whether they like me or they hate me, just tell somebody."

Still, 50 also felt confident about the album's chances for success based on the work he had invested in its recording, explaining that "I think (the record sounds) great. I think I'm going to really impress people who have been listening to me up until this point. I would be nervous right now if I had a weak record with all of this hype going on."

"Get Rich or Die Trying" was released nationally on Friday, February 6, 2003, four days before the traditional Tuesday album release, in an unusual industry move designed to combat the very bootleg/mixtape market that had given 50 the street buzz he was riding high on. With a major label debut that entered (not surprisingly) at # 1 on the Billboard Top 200 Album Chart, 50 Cent sold 872,000 copies nationally in his first week as a major label artist, and would go onto sell 1.7 million copies of 'Get Rich by the end of its second week in release.

Ultimately, the record would sell upward of 4.3 million copies in just 12 weeks, rivaling only mentors Eminem and the late Tupac Shakur in soundscan's record books for a hip hop release. Reflecting on the album's sensational success only a few months after its release, in the late spring of 2003, 50 admitted that, despite his confidence on tape and in the media regarding his rise to hip hop's premier spot, "I didn't anticipate selling that many records…I sold 872,000 copies my first week. It's almost normal for artists to drop like 35 percent in sales the following week. I came back and did 822,000 the next week, so I was shocked."

The rest of the record buying world, however, was not, and couldn't get enough of 50-Mania. While the Dr. Dre-produced first single 'In Da Club' shot to the top of the Billboard Pop Singles Chart, and remained there for weeks, 50 quickly followed up with '21 Questions', which quickly joined its predecessor in the top 10, giving 50 Cent 2 top ten singles simultaneously, a new record for a debut hip hop artist. MTV rotated 50's videos more times than the rims on the fleet of cars he rolled in throughout the videos for both songs. His scheduling was so insane between interviews, live shows, remix-vocal recordings, and 50's related promotional commitments that he had to shoot the videos for '21 Questions' and the album's third single, 'Many Men', back to back in March of 2003, a mere month after the album's release.

For 50's part, he enjoyed staying busy, explaining to one journalist that "my schedule is consistent. I got a show every day, so it didn't really bother me shooting two videos. Actually, in the middle of that I had to go and do a concert, then I had to fly back and complete the visuals. We shot both of them in 5 days…I'm workin, Its nothing new! This is my first album and I'm a new artist to the world, but I've been around for a long time!"

Being a team player, 50 was also quick to credit both of his immediate label bosses, Eminem and Dr. Dre, not only with providing him the insular support he needed on the label side to blow up like he did, but also for allowing him to be an entrepreneur amidst it all with plans to start his own label, G-Unit, owned and distributed independently of any stake on Em or Dre's part, outside of his solo contract. This allowed 50 the opportunity to begin developing a catalog, testing his own A&R instincts with the G-Unit crew he put on via his imprint of the same namesake, and in the midst of it all, setting an example for younger emcees by thinking ahead of his immediate success, planning for the future after his popularity as a solo artist had perhaps subsided, a reality which potentially faces all hit rappers, just as it does major-league athletes, in a parallel example.

Still, in spite of the independence of his label deal with G-Unit, that 50 was still under the Interscope Records umbrella along Dre and Em, each with their own respective labels, made the rapper feel part of a true hip hop dynasty, boasting that "Aftermath is loaded, like you got alotta great essence.. You got Ice Cube, Rakim, you got new artist Joe Beast, new artist Brooklyn, that's on aftermath but there's some more acts I'm not really familiar with.. Shady is Eminem, D-12, Obie Trice and I'm kinda splittin between the two, cause my deal is a joint between Shady and Aftermath...I could be in there and be the guy under (Eminem and Dre), or I can make myself almost the equivalent of them."

"That's what I'm working to do—you know the other rappers aren't exciting right now to me." Ultimately, 50 felt he had little to worry about in terms of the security of his deal with Interscope, namely because, by his logic, "when you do business with people who [are scared of you] they don't play games with you." One area 50 proved to have a ready expertise in was that of guerilla marketing, developed mainly out of his years reinventing himself on the mixtape circuit after the failed deal with Columbia and his near-fatal shooting, explaining that "absolutely (I'm involved with all of album's street-level marketing), everything you see on the streets. I feel like I'm a marketing person now."

With the massive media attention paid to 50 Cent based on his record-setting album sales and refreshing aura of authenticity, he was forced, to some degree, to open up with journalists on topics that weren't directly related to his hustling background and its related exploits. In some cases, he was asked about his musical tastes, which like 50's admission that he did not drink or do drugs, came as a surprise even to the journalist, as well as his fans, "I listen to music people probably don't believe I listen to. Nirvana's 'Teen Spirit', I love that record. The melodies are ridiculous. I like Maroon5's 'Harder to Breathe.' That's dope. I like the White Stripes' single ('Seven Nation Army'.) There could be a hip-hop version of that. But the album is too rock for me."

Similarly, within context of surprising answers, while 50 rapped readily and frequently about his faith in God on record, he added the of his own inner vulnerability and insecurity regarding how he will be viewed on judgment day, explaining that despite his bold raps regarding past criminal exploits, "I don't go to church every Sunday, but I believe in God, and I pray. When I catch myself thinking negative things for no reason, I say a prayer so I'm forgiven for it. I fear that some of my actions won't be understood (by God)."

Along with the process of revealing all sides of 50's rather intricate and brilliant personality, inevitable given the insatiable media focus on him, 50 would be offered the opportunity to reveal even more of his person to the world, in a different medium entirely from hip hop. As is somewhat requisite by present-day industry standards, when a hot new rapper blows up, they must do a semi-autobiographical movie, hence Eminem with '8 Mile' (which coincidentally had introduced the broader hip hop world to 50 Cent on the movie's soundtrack).

For 50's part, he seemed more eager to tour and record new material than to rush right into a movie, following Eminem's lead in taking his time picking a script, and prepping for whatever would end up being his debut film role, reasoning that "I'm gonna explore all my options and film opportunities, but I'm not in a hurry…I'm gonna wait till I can do films as well as I can rap."

In the more immediate time, 50 set out on the road in the summer of 2003, embarking on his first co-headlining arena tour with former rival Jay-Z from the days of 'How to Rob.' These days, the two emcees preferred to be partners in crime, stealing the summer's number one buzz spot with their 30+ city tour, which also featured veterans Snoop Dogg and Busta Rhymes opening for 50 Cent.

Already a veteran of the club concert stage, 50 found no difficulties translating his live set to the arena stage, describing his philosophy and approach to achieving a crowd-pleasing live set as one in which "I got like a favorite six records…It's the first six records I perform: 'What Up Gangsta,' 'Wanksta,' 'Back Down,' 'High All the Time,' 'In Da Club,' and 'P.I.M.P.' It's the way you set up and how you position the show." Still, in the presence of the tour's headlining act, 50 preferred to be a happy student.

Opening for living hip-hop legend Jay-Z, clearly the star attraction for most audiences by night's end, allowed 50 to see what mastery of a live hip hop audience was all about from hip hop's pinnacle, explaining to MTV.com that "Jay's a different type of performer. Jay's probably the coolest guy live. He's not gonna sweat, he's not gonna move. He pulled a G move on me last night. He got up an (slowly raised and waved his hands, beckoning the crowd.) That's experience from him being around and knowing that (a simple move like that is) effective. Ahead of him doing that, he had no movement. So the crowd was looking around waiting for him to do something. Then when he did something they knew to respond."

While 50 held his own with the crowd every night, he seemed to be taking notes on everybody who was part of the bill, even hip hop staples who were opening for him, in spite of being around for years prior, "every night Busta (Rhymes) is probably one of the most charismatic guys onstage. He'll come out and be like 'Yo May! If you just change (up the order of your songs), if you do that song in front of that record right there, its a wrap! I don't see how anybody is gonna be able to survive out here.' I switched up too. I'm learning, I'm open to anybody's suggestions as long as it makes sense to me...I watch alot of these niggas, that's how you learn."

Following the wildly successful 'Roc-the-Mic' tour, 50 Cent returned to New York to continue work on what would be his crew (and label of the same name) G-Unit's debut LP. In addition, he would begin the process of collecting the official accolades of the fans and industry via an endless string of award shows that would begin with the 2003 MTV Video Music Awards in September, 2003, where 50 collected 2 awards won for Best Rap Video and Best New Artist, and continue throughout the fall with a host of others, collecting various trophies from the BET Awards, the World Music Awards, the Source Awards, the Radio Music Awards, the VIBE Music Awards, and the American Music Awards. He would end 2003 with 6.5 million copies of his debut LP sold, and a vote by the readers of *Rolling Stone Magazine* as Best New Artist. He would begin 2004 nominated for 5 of the record industry's most prestigious awards, the Grammys, including Best New Artist.

Non-stop make it hot, we the top regardless
You can be the hardest, we'll just be the smartest
I warn you not to start us, we're not your average artists...
You betta get used to it, you know how we do it
Shady, Aftermath, Interscope and G-Unit
We got action when you don't
Show our faces when you won't
G-Unit, G-G-G-G, G-Unit
G-Unit, G-Unit 2004

Chapter 11
G-Unit

As 50 ascended overnight to the top of hip hop, it came as no surprise that he had a crew to bring along with him. The G-Unit consisted of Young Buck, Tony Yayo and Lloyd Banks, and would quickly distinguish themselves from other crews that had come before them because they could actually rap. This was in part due to the unique fact that G-Unit wasn't only composed of 50's childhood friends, but also legitimate emcees that he collected from around the country into what would become hip hop's next multi-platinum clique.

As 50 explained the make-up of G-Unit to one journalist while he was still in the process of shopping a deal for his own label, it was clear he was operating from the mindset of his mentors Eminem and Dr. Dre, seeking to build upon his own momentum in the present to plan for the future, "G Unit is my record company, it is a group at this point because the deal is about to complete the negotiations. G-Unit is a beautiful thing to me. I put LLoyd Banks and Tony YaYo on. We grew up together like, Banks is the youngest he's 20 years old. I signed them a year and a half ago… when I was in the middle of shopping for my deal. I had deals [on the table], but this is my third record deal, so I wanted to [sign] the right deal."

"I was really patient. Universal had a label for me for G-Unit after the first mixtape went out. They heard it on the street and saw how far it was actually going. I wasn't really interested in the deal because of Universal as a company. Universal has so many talented artists there that they just throw balls against the wall. If they stick, it's a hit, if it doesn't, move to the next one. G Unit is new…it's hard to break an entire crew or entire situation, and it's starting to come along… we laid the groundwork so I'm happy to see the progress…We in negotiations now, (the label) should be distributed by Interscope. If they give me the right bag of money or it might be someone else, depending on Jimmy (Iovine)."

Proving to be predictably shrewd, Interscope gave 50 the deal he wanted, and G-Unit Records was born. While 50 as a solo artist remained signed to Shady/Aftermath, G-Unit as a clique, as well as any other artist 50 chose to put on, were signed independently under his control, allowing the rapper an extremely rare entrepreneurial opportunity for a freshman recording artist. Knowing that 50's stamp on any project he released through G-Unit would be a guaranteed platinum endeavor, Iovine and Interscope were in essence betting on a sure thing.

50's first project under the G-Unit banner was an album by his crew of the same name, wherein he was so confident in the group's potential for commercial breakthrough that he stopped work on his own follow-up to Get Rich or Die Tryin' to work on the group's debut LP. According to fellow G-Unit member Lloyd Banks, the album's recording was "competitive, especially 50...I didn't really have to look outside the studio for that drive. I go in the studio and Yayo's got a verse that's making me go, 'Whoa! I gotta go do something else.'"

Echoing his bandmate's sentiment, Tony Yayo nevertheless expressed support for his fellow G-Unit members, explaining that "of course we're competitive, 'cause that keeps you on your toes...Banks has damn near the hottest punch lines in New York. He'll say a hot punch line and I'll be like, 'How the fuck did you say that?' Banks has always been talented. Then here comes 50 with some fire and then I know I gotta write some shit. 50 could go in the booth and do a song in two minutes. 50 knows how to make songs. He knows how to make hits."

According to G-Unit Records artist Game, the creative level in the studio among 50 and his labelmates was reminiscent of that during the recording of the legendary 'Chronic' LP by Dr. Dre and his Death Row Records co-hearts over a decade earlier. Perhaps among the most concentrated new stables of talent to emerge in recent years, the artists on G-Unit all appeared to have one another's backs in the studio just as they might on the street corners, using that hustler comradery to create what would prove to be one of the most authentic gangsta rap group albums since N.W.A's 'Straight Outta Compton', as Game continued, "When we all in the studio, it's like just crazy creativity...These are MCs that are all street and they all bring something different to the table. Then when they jell, you never have a problem, you never catch writer's block. You feed off one another and that's what we try to do when we in there. It's usually 50 that's more creative, cause he's real melody-driven. It's usually him coming up with the song format. Then after that it's just me, Banks and Buck that takes it. Now that Yayo's home it just adds more base to a foundation that's already in its mold. It's crazy man, it's like it's easy. We're knocking out three songs in a matter of an hour and a half."

Label head 50 Cent was perhaps the most enthusiastic about his new protégés, so much so that he not only delayed the release of his sophomore album for Shady/Aftermath, but seemed to have his label, Interscope, equally as enthused, "I was gonna release it in the first quarter, but (the label) asked me to give (G-Unit's Beg for Mercy) room, you know…The material for (the G-Unit) record came out so well, they feel like it's gonna (have a long shelf life)…I haven't heard anything negative about my music the entire time (my record's been out)…The G-Unit album is tough. People are not fair so they're going to make it (seem like) it's my second album. I had to work extra hard on this album (and) now I'm content with them calling this my second album. I think its good enough."

Feeling that 50's fans would best embrace the G-Unit debut if they felt it was on the level of 'Get Rich or Die Trying', as their debut album's release date approached, 50's group adopted a similar spin in the media regarding the album's continuity with 50's solo debut. Moreover, the members of the G-Unit went out of their way to paint their group as part of a larger extended family of superstars, as G-Unit member Young Buck explained, "The album is crazy…We have production by Eminem (and) Dr. Dre. We worked with a lot of different upcoming producers like Emil, Alchemist and DJ Twinz. We didn't really get too many features—we kept it G-Unit. Basically what you got from 'Get Rich or Die Tryin' is the same thing you can look forward to on the G-Unit album or maybe more. We got a lot of stuff in store." Lloyd Banks echoed Young Buck, explaining that "it's like a sequel to 'Get Rich or Die Tryin' as far as the quality of music." Reassuring fans that they had been working in the studio night and day alongside 50 to create hip hop's next prodigal LP, Banks continued in elaboration on the album's recording, assuring fans that "we're all workaholics…I went from making two records a week to making three records at a time, every time I (went) into the studio."

"You could be asleep, wake up with an idea and have a record before you know it. Most of the record we have came from playing around…If you hear something in your head more than 10 times, nines times out of 10 it's gonna be a record. It comes out good because we was together." As 50 used his own overnight popularity to introduce the world to G-Unit by taking his crew on tour in the summer of 2003, they would routinely step off-stage and onto the tour bus with the record button on their state-of-the-art digital studio blinking in wait.

As such, according to Lloyd Banks, much of the album was recorded on the road, reflecting the group's focus and work-a-holic attitude toward making it, "Yeah, we were on the Rock the Mic Tour, you know, with a whole bunch of other guys—Jay-Z, Snoop, a bunch of popular people. We had a studio on the bus so it was kinda cool…Man, the process of working on this album was work, then some more work… And some more work, a little bit of play, a little bit of sleep. For the most part it was work, but it was a cool experience."

Adding his own endorsement icing to what was sure to be cake for all involved, 50 explained that everyone in the Shade/Aftermath/G-Unit/Interscope extended family was feeling the pressure since they all had financial interests in the album's success, "(its not just us.) There's pressure on Dr. Dre, also…He has to produce a better record for me than 'In Da Club.'"

Leaving predictions on the album's performance largely up to the G-Unit new comers, Young Buck took care of covering the requisite cocky confidence required on the part of any new rap act, boasting that he felt the album would easily sell "a million and a half copies," going on to erase any notion of limitations by predicting fans wouldn't have a choice once the word of mouth got started nationally, "I believe anything is possible. You know, with the controversy around the album… Basically, I think it's real life behind the album and the controversy behind the album."

"There's a lot of things that 50 Cent, Lloyd Banks, Young Buck and Tony Yayo are saying on that album that's gonna make you stop and say, 'Hold up—I know they didn't just say that.' It's gonna draw a whole lot more people." Of course, G-Unit's debut LP, 'Beg For Mercy', charted the number 3 spot in the Billboard Top 200 Album chart in its first week (abbreviated to 3 days of a normal 7 day calendar week to combat bootleggers), moving 376,000 copies, and reminiscent of 50's debut, went onto sell 2 million copies in its first months of release.

Building on the instant success of G-Unit's debut LP, 50 and company were already well underway with the work on the first solo album from the crew, by Lloyd Banks, who 50 went about introducing individually to fans via the G-Unit LP. For his part, Banks was ready to compete with, and/or exceed the success of his boss's debut album in terms of both quality and caliber of the material, explaining that "I knew I could make records, but I ain't wanna tell them that. For what?…I wanted it to build up for now."

"On my album there's everything—the hook, the bridges, the character, everything is coming out. They'll get a good feel of who Lloyd Banks is and what I could bring to the table. 50 came out last year and blew by everybody like the roadrunner. I plan on doing the same thing…I got damn near 60 records in preparation for my album. I got my drive from 50. I know when he gets a rush. I know when its a go. If he doesn't go crazy when I play a song for him, then I scrap that one. I have alot of faith in him."

Lloyd Banks first hooked up with 50 Cent out of high school in 1999, at the tender age of 17. Bearing many similarities to his mentor, including the fact that they both hailed from Southside Queens, New York, and that in 2001, Banks was himself shot twice in an attempt on his life. As Banks elaborated on his background with 50, "I grew up in south side Queens; me and Yayo lived on the same street and 50 lived around the corner."

"I'm the youngest, 50 is older than me and I've been rapping for a long time. The stuff I was rapping about…I wasn't going through the things that 50 was going through at the time, I was young, in junior high school. I wasn't really into the street, and 50 was older, he was already in the street. Me and Yayo were going through things that were totally different because we were closer in age. So as we got older our experiences changed… Then 50 got shot and when he got shot a lot of people turned their back on him."

"A lot of your friends stay away because they don't know if whoever shot you the first time is going to come back and try it again. So a lot of true colors come through. And I had gotten shot too so I was in the same frame of mind as him, so I rode with him. I was like, 'Man, if I can get into the rap game.' The rap game is like the crack game, you're taking the street approach to the game, not everything is done by the book. So I thought if I'm going to get into a business where it's shady and things can happen, I'm gonna get into it with somebody who would take it with me, and vice versa."

"So you know, this is genuine, this is not something that was put together, we grew up together. If we were on the block hustling, we would ALL be on the block hustling. If we were stealing cars, we'd be stealing cars together. That's what separates G-Unit from a lot of the groups out there." Taking Banks under his wing, 50 began to hone the rapper's skills in the studio and featured him on mix tape after mix tape, alongside fellow protégé Tony Yayo, who ended up in prison on a weapon's charge in December, 2002, prior to the release of either 50 Cent or G-Unit's debut LPs.

While his crew had Yayo's back, they focused in more immediate terms on the pending release of Banks' debut, 'Hungry for More', which sold competitively with G-Unit's debut LP on its street date of June 29, 2004, moving 434,000 copies in its first week, and debuting at number 1 on the Billboard Top 200 Album chart. Over the course of the summer of 2004, the album would sell upward of a million copies.

Still, 50 and the boys didn't stop there, prepping Young Buck's debut, 'Straight Outta Cashville', for a fall 2004 release, and equally as optimistic at the prospect for its platinum potential, as

Buck boasted to an MTV.com journalist, explaining that his album would be "just like 'Straight Outta Compton', but for y'all that don't know what Cashville is, it's short for Nashville...I'm from the Dirty Dirty, so I kinda brought a few Southern artists into the picture...We in the kitchen cooking. It's extra, extra, extra well done."

Interestingly, in hailing from the south, Young Buck was first discovered and put on by Cash Money Records star Juvenile before hooking up with 50's G-Unit clique. As he explained why he ended up with 50, Buck explained that "basically, I was runnin' with Juvenile, and he was in the process of trying to get his own label started, UTP Records. Everything wasn't really moving as planned, but you know, it was moving. And one day he happened to just go to New York, looking to do some recording and trying to put together a new deal for his company."

"I was kinda like the guy who was riding with Juvie, trying to make things happen. He was like, 'Yo man, I think I can get in touch with 50.' And it just ended up happening. And at the time Juvenile had a studio on the bus, and 50 came by, Banks, Yayo. We started like a little side project on the bus and it was not no battle thing, but just spittin' individually. The kid was feeling Buck, and I was feeling the kid from the beginning, I always knew who 50 Cent was, I never had a chance to really touch base with him."

"So when I got a chance to meet him, I spilled all my beans to him and let him know what situation I was in, where I was coming from. And 50 Cent basically kept it real, like, 'Yo, if this rap thing happens for me man, I'm gonna come back and holler.' And that's exactly what he did." The results have spoke for themselves, and commercially, will likely continue to with the pending release of Young Buck's debut.

Only 50's oldest friend within the G-Unit crew, Tony Yayo, missed out on much of the 50 Cent and G-Unit hoopla that dominated 2003 and 2004, namely because he was serving time in prison on bail jumping and weapons charges. Still, his crew stayed loyal, shouting out to Yayo often on the G-Unit debut, wearing 'Free Yayo' T-shirts to award shows and related promotional appearances, featuring the rapper in an interview from Riker's Island on the group's highly successful DVD release in the summer of 2003, while 50 and the suits at Interscope worked behind the scenes to secure his release, and paid his legal bills.

Upon his release from Lakeview Shock Incarceration Correctional Facility in January, 2004, Yayo was thrown a welcome home party by New York's Hot 97.1, and presented with keys to a new home and set of wheels, courtesy of 50 and his G-Unit crew, as well as label G-Unit/Interscope. Unfortunately, Yayo's taste of freedom would be short-lived when he was almost immediately picked up for a parole violation by possessing a fake passport. Taken into Federal Custody, it would take Interscope's legal machine 5 months and thousands of dollars to secure Yayo's second release from jail.

Still, in the few days he was out of prison in January, 2004, Yayo would record 12 songs in the studio toward his debut LP, and following 5 months of additional incarceration throughout the spring of 2004. In June, Yayo was re-released from Federal Custody after pleading guilty to the charge of possessing a false passport, an odd charge he explained away as a situation in which "when I was on the run, I went and got a passport made. Me and my brother kinda look alike. So I went and got a passport made so I could be on the run—'cause I wanted to fly to Barcelona. I wanted to fly around the world." Upon release, Yayo's attorney Scott Leeman sought to reassure the powers that be that Yayo's illegal world-traveling days were behind him, commenting that "today's plea should be the culmination of Tony's problems with the law…Tony realizes that he is now in the public spotlight, and now, more than ever, he welcomes and understands the responsibilities that come with fame. One of the most important responsibilities is accepting responsibility for one's wrongdoing, which Tony has done here."

Yayo left the courthouse and proceeded directly to the studio to continue work on his pending debut LP. While his attorney professed contrition on Yayo's part, the G-Unit co-founder, for his own part, was more boastful (and seemed subtly flippant), expressing his appreciation for 50's support, and largely dismissing the seriousness of the charge he was locked up for, explaining that "it feels good to come home to a million dollars in the account, you know? I didn't really do anything, and I got a million dollars in my account, so it feels beautiful...My boy 50 took care of me, so I know the love is there. Usually, when a person's in a bad predicament, their people ain't gonna look out for them. But me? I had to tell 50 to stop sending me money!...I didn't feel left out because everywhere you go, you see 'Free Yayo'...It just excited me to see Em with a 'Free Yayo,' shirt. You see 50 with the 'Free Yayo' campaign going on in the videos. They didn't forget about me."

Once out of prison, Yayo had no problem playing catch-up with his other G-Unit members, hitting hip hop hot spot 'Jacob the Jewelers' in New York to splurge on Jewelry, and buying himself two new whips, including a Bentley and a Porsche Cayenne. Regarding any affect prison may have had on his inherent focus or abilities as a recording artist, Yayo explained that being locked down while his crew blew up gave him hope and only "made me hungrier. I knew success was gonna come. 50's a star. (Lloyd) Banks is a star. I'm a star. Young Buck's a star. Everybody's a star. I'm on the dream team. We got Dre, we got Em. There's no way we're gonna lose."

If nothing else, Yayo's incarceration and the media attention it received only worked to maintain if not strengthen 50's crew's authenticity in the street, and keep fans anxious for Yayo's release, both from prison and into stores. For his part, as the summer of 2004 progressed and Lloyd Banks blew up as a solo artist, Tony Yayo was only encouraged by the success of his fellow G-Unit group member, telling MTV.com news that "I'm just working...I got an album done already—in 12 days. I just hope 50 is OK with it."

"Whatever he likes, he likes. Whatever he don't like, he scraps it...I think my lyrics right now are gonna reflect the prison system. My album is just gonna be street, gonna be 'hood. I'm trying to make the crime rate go up...I feel I'm getting better and better. I'm more focused. This is really what I like doing. I feel like I should've been doing this (all along). I was bullshit in the 'hood. (Now) I wake up every day excited."

Conclusion
Better Days

As 50 continued his rule of hip hop, both as a label head and artist in his own right, part of his victory came through persevering past beefs that had threatened to bring him down in the beginning of his career. His strategy for success, aside from a relentless work ethic, had been simply to keep-it-real, even as the money began rolling in. While this paid off handsomely for 50, things had not panned out so well for arguably his biggest rival, Murder Inc., whose flagship artist, 50 nemesis Ja Rule's, last two albums, 2003's Blood in My Eye, and 2004's R.U.L.E., had both flopped commercially, failing to sell more than a million copies collectively. More seriously however, on a personal level, on January 26th, 2005, label C.E.O. Irv Gotti, along with his brother Chris, were arrested by the F.B.I. and charged with money laundering.

According to *USA Today*, "the hip-hop label behind music superstars Ashanti and Ja Rule was part of a murderous criminal enterprise that protected its interstate crack and heroin operation with calculated street assassinations, federal authorities charged Wednesday…Label head Irv "Gotti" Lorenzo and his brother Christopher surrendered to the FBI on money-laundering charges Wednesday as federal prosecutors unsealed an indictment seeking to confiscate all the assets of their label, The Inc…Their childhood friend, Kenneth "Supreme" McGriff, one of New York's most notorious drug kingpins, was charged with murder, racketeering and other crimes that prosecutors said were intended to eliminate and intimidate potential witnesses…He already is in prison on a relatively minor gun charge...Prosecutors believe McGriff and the Lorenzos funneled hundreds of thousands of dollars in drug profits through The Inc., a chart-topping label owned partly by Island Def Jam, a Universal Music label...Federal agents began to close in on McGriff and the Lorenzos in recent months with arrests that netted Ja Rule's manager and a book-keeper for The Inc. At least five other defendants, including associates of McGriff, already have been charged....McGriff, 44, was founder of the Supreme Team, once one of the city's most violent drug crews. Investigators suspect that after he finished serving about nine years for drug conspiracy in 1997, he set about reviving his lucrative—and deadly—drug-dealing operation... Cooperating witnesses have told investigators that McGriff admitted to the 2001 revenge slaying of up-and-coming rapper E-Money Bags. Prosecutors also believe he arranged the Baltimore killing one month later of a suspected informant in his drug organization. Another man also died in the Baltimore shooting."

MTV.com news, in elaborating on the indictment, reported that "after the hearing, Irv Gotti made a brief statement. 'I'm gonna give you guys one comment. I want to make it very crystal clear that I don't look (badly) at the government in any way, shape or form for them thinking I'm doing anything wrong. I call myself Gotti, I made my label Murder Inc., I grew up poor, from the street. But I don't look bad at them for thinking ill things of me. In no way have I done anything wrong except make great music that people seem to love. That's all I'm guilty of.'...New York City Police Commissioner Raymond Kelly said at a press conference Wednesday afternoon that 'They don't call it gangsta rap for nothing — the thug image isn't accidental...This is not an indictment of rap music. If you're involved with money laundering or drug dealing or committing murder, we're coming after you, irrespective of (the music). That's our business.'...The assets of McGriff's companies, Picture Perfect Films and Picture Perfect Enterprises, have been seized; their combined worth is approximately

$425,000. Authorities are seeking to seize the assets of the Inc. and the affiliated IG Records as well...McGriff, along with eight associates, has been indicted for racketeering, illegal use of fire-arms, drug distribution and homicide. The associates include Inc. bookkeeper Cynthia Brent, who was arrested on money-launder-ing charges in November and released on a $200,000 bond; Ja Rule's manager, Ron 'Gutta' Robinson; Vash-Ti Paylor; Nicole Brown; Dennis 'Divine' Crosby; and Victor Wright."

For 50's part, his final commentary on the Gotti beef was one in which "I think it's sad (about) Irv Gotti's situation. He's the guy who allowed his blessings to turn into something negative. After establishing himself in the music business, he tried to become something he never had the heart to be in his neighborhood. That's where "Gotti" came from. He was DJ Irv ahead of that. Anybody that's in the street is trying to get out. You can't blame anyone but Irv." 50, surprisingly, had less harsh words for Ja Rule, sympathetically stating that "I might sign Ja Rule when he's done at Murder Inc. After I destroy him, I'll rebuild him."

Beginning in early 2004, 50 Cent began work on his highly-antic-ipated follow-up to Get Rich and Die Tryin. Slated for a mid-Feb-ruary release, the album was initially entitled 'The St. Valentines Day Massacre', although, according to 50, the only battle he was having on street date was "competing with myself... Anything less than 11 million records would be a failure, I'm talking about the end of the record. With the first album I felt like I failed because anything I was doing, I was doing for the first time. I know what I'm doing this time, last time I was like 'ok, what am I supposed to do?' and I didn't really know...If there were something else going on that would excite me. I have to use Em as my balance. In his career he continues to go uphill. And I feel like that's what's hap-pening to me. I surround myself with the kind of people that I can accept criticism from. Everyone has an opinion. But I don't accept everyone's opinion. I know Em and Dre are in my best interest. I respect them and I listen to them. In so many ways Em gets me excited about things that no one else can get me excited about."

"I was on my DVD for The New Breed before I came out with Get Rich Or Die Tryin' and they asked me what do I fear. I said I fear not fitting in with Eminem and Dr. Dre. All of these other issues in the street and you fear not fitting in? I said, yes because all of those things are the norm from where I come from and this is the new exciting thing for me to be able to fit in with them. I've been progressing at a pace that I think is cool but I can progress at an even faster pace. They should look forward to me releasing even more material that has the same quality over a shorter time span than last time. I had to wait. I set Banks and Buck up with Beg For Mercy and then they released their solo projects. I don't have to wait any more."

In fact, 50 would have to wait, just a bit longer, while his next G-Unit superstar—The GAME—blew up in the same big-bang that 50 had come out of the gate with, in a move 50 explained as one in which "I had to move it back because of my Game record…(I'm) not disappointed because I'll still be able to use a lot of things I had planned for it but I really did want a release on February 15th… I was trying to force Interscope Records to release my record on February 15, but Interscope Records is reactive. I'm proactive, so I threw 'Disco Inferno' out and kinda got them to respond to me. But (The Massacre) probably wouldn't even be coming out March 8 if I didn't do that at that point, because this project is a big project to them, they want to have everything mapped out and it's more mechanical this time."

When he wasn't in the studio, 50 followed his mentors Eminem and Dr. Dre into the boardroom, launching G-Unit Records into an active label, releasing albums by Lloyd Banks, Young Buck, and in early 2005, The Game. The latter emcee, hailing from Compton, California, was brought into 50's fold at the suggestion of Interscope chief Jimmy Iovine, much in the way he had first brought Eminem to the attention of Dr. Dre years before.

While the Game was signed officially to G-Unit through After-math, and was motivated for his own part, as a Compton native, by the opportunity to work with Dr. Dre. The teaming with 50 Cent in a mentoring relationship followed the tried-and-true for-mula that had worked first for Dr. Dre and Eminem, and then for Eminem and 50 Cent, and secured the Game instant credibility with the record buying public on a national level. As 50 Cent rea-soned, "I think it's interesting to see how (the public will) embrace the (Game's) record since he's coming from the West Coast... What I been trying to do is diversify the perception and the vibe of G-Unit. This is another artist who speaks about another environ-ment, being from Los Angeles, but he's aggressive also."

In terms of 50's relationship personally with the Game in contrast to fellow G-Unit crew mates Lloyd Banks, Young Buck, and Tony Yayo, 50 explained that "we have a different relationship, I've known Lloyd Banks and Tony Yayo all my life, Young Buck isn't so closely into the camp, he's spent the last 2 years around me. So it will take time for me and Game to develop the same relationship that me and the rest of the crew have but he's a part of the crew like everybody else and I want to add it to you that his first week sales just came and he sold 586,933 records...Game's first week, it's exciting for me to have an artist come out and go gold the first week, especially when Ja Rule's record is out there and he's at 538,000 records right now. Game's sold more than Ja Rule in his first week after his album's been on sale for 10 weeks."

For the Game's part, he explained that "I opted for Aftermath since Dre was from Compton, I'm from Compton, you know... I'll keep the whole N.W.A legacy going....That's where I wanted to be...Dr. Dre, he got his own way, his order of operations that he likes to have...And he had the successes of Snoop Dogg, then Eminem, then 50 Cent, then myself coming up, batting cleanup. He got the magic, man. At the end of the day, I wouldn't be nothing without Dre's beats. Without Dre's (and 50's) tutelage and (them) mentoring me for the last two-and-a-half years we wouldn't be standing out here doing this interview and I'd probably be part of the crowd and somebody else would be talking to you."

With the Game's release safely in the bag, 50 Cent throughout the month of January and the early part of February, continued last minute touch-ups on what he hoped would be his masterpiece, such that "The Massacre, I think it's better than Get Rich or Die Tryin', honestly...I spent a lot of time, put a lot of details into it. I actually took longer recording this record than I did Get Rich or Die Tryin'...When I started, I went in and did like 14, 15 records...Then I put those records aside and started over. I went out to L.A. and worked with Dre. We got some special joints so I'm excited right now. I know I'm gonna exceed everyone's expectations on this project because they feel like Get Rich or Die Tryin' was the best I could do. I got something up my sleeve."

Elaborating on their collaboration in the studio, Dr. Dre explained that, the second time out, "it is pretty much the same technique—we go in, I have some tracks ready and he just comes in and does his thing...I think the last time we worked (it took) what, about a week?...We just worked about a week on the record and I think we put in about two weeks this time...You know what's going to happen—it is going to be crazy."

50's confidence in his sophomore effort secure based on the inclusion of Dre's sure-platinum fire beats, the rapper boasted that "I guarantee this album will be 10 times better than my first record. It's a little more complex. Now that I know people are listening, I can articulate and write the things I wanna write. My first record, I was just trying to have fun with it and express my actual situations. I write about the harsh realities. I'm just interested in seeing how they respond to it."

Elaborating on the making of his new album, 50 explained that "it's a continuation from Get Rich or Die Trying; I took a photograph and added illustrations to it. It got a flip-off cover and then there's a whole other artwork. It's exciting cause what I did for my album insert is I picked photographs to go inside with the lyrical content of some of the songs to give you a visual of what I'm saying. You know, I listen to the music when I buy a CD and I stare at the pictures so what I do is I make the pictures actually feel like they're tied to the songs…There's (also) some major differences between these records."

"I went back, I put the things that I missed on Get Rich Or Die Trying and I added a lot of details. I feel like this record is better than Get Rich Or Die Trying. I can't wait to see how the general public embraces it…(The producers on the record include) Eminem, Dr Dre, Scott Storch, Hi-Tek, Needlz, Buckwild, 4 or 5 new producers cause when I listen to the beats, I have (people) take off the names of where the music came from, so when I listen to it, I'm just listening to it for the music, not for who made it…When they send me music, I have them send it to me with no label on it. All I'm listening to is music. I'm listening to it with fresh ears. I'm not being altered because Neptunes made it. Sometimes that changes your perception of the record. You'll want it to be good. Because of who made it…"

"Even on this project you'll see a lot of new guys, various production. On Beg For Mercy it was like that too. At the end we recorded four songs with Dre. We had one day in LA…We took full advantage of it. All four of the records went on the album…I recorded 11 records in 3 days, I really did! And then I kept 4 of 'em cause I felt they were a good representation of me, from Get Rich Or Die Trying till now. But the records are great so in the future you'll probably hear some of those records…One of my favorite songs is A Baltimore Love Thing…It's titled that because in Baltimore the heroin addiction rate is really high. So the song is about the relationship between an addict and the drug. I give this drug a motion, feelings and at some point in the song, the drug actually becomes mad at the addict for trying to leave. It's like a real vivid description of what it would be like if it was human...You hear people make references to drugs-talking and people who are addicted to it."

"So what I did is I created a song where I'm actually the drug talking to the person...I don't have an A&R department when it comes to my project," he explained. "I get so personal with it that I've got to kind of pick everything myself. So I have them take the music that's sent to us and have them put it onto a blank CD and just put a number on the CD instead of just sending me the name of the actual producer. Sometimes you lean toward music that is produced by a great producer, someone that you have respect for, and you may pick something that ain't actually the hottest thing."

50's first single for the new album, 'Disco Inferno', was released in late December, 2004, and by mid-January, 2005, had cracked the top 5 on Billboard's Top 200 Singles Chart. 50, for his part, was visibly excited about the public response to his first single off the new album, as well as the second single, 'Candy Shop', remarking that "the record's done incredible... It's #4 in the country right now, and it had zero support from Interscope Records. I went out with it with or without them and they caught up to it."

"They ended up sending (out official promos) after I MP3ed it across the country. I feel good about it, and now I'm ready to move into The Candy Shop...It's a little...it's edgy...I think the song itself is great...I attempted to be as sexual as possible, from a male perspective, without being vulgar or obscene. I think that I did a great job on it. The video itself, visually, me and (director) Jessy Terrero came up with the treatment for. It's exciting. Trick Daddy had a song (Sugar) that he put out where he had candy references in the video, so I didn't go that route, and we tried to do something a little different... I'm really excited; I can't wait to see how the general public embraces my album. I'm just ready now; I've sat already long enough, almost 2 years."

50 hadn't exactly been sitting around. In addition to building his record label, which the rapper displayed a fantastically realistic

attitude about in the context of longevity, despite G-Unit Records' wildly successful first year out, 50 reasoned—with impressive business acumen—that "you know, it's difficult enough to have the proper staffing, it's not easy to have knowledgeable people and it's expensive. And you need to have connections so you gotta come with the money. So, independently, when you come out, you can't just jump into that seat and then become a major. Look at majors as National Saving Banks. They got the money in order to allow you to create new projects. And the more success you have with them, the more finance they'll give you. When you do a subsidiary they kinda give you a 50 percent profit split and what that is they'll give you the money to make the project, cover the expenses to actually create the product and after they get their money back and you split the profits."

So if you took yourself away from that, you have to have all the money upfront to make the record, to market it, all the money to transport the artists-flying, hotels, cabs, limousines and you need to pay your staff at the same time. I mean, I'll be a major, I think G-Unit ain't Interscope records, it's just 2 years old, and Interscope is 13 years old." What made the triple-threat of Dre, Em and 50 work on a corporate and commercial level, according to Eminem, was a team strategy in which "Dre is the coach and I'm playing quarterback and 50 is the receiver, he's the go-to man right now."

"Everyone is set up in a place to play that position and it's more important for us to win overall, you know. It's about winning the championship as opposed to any individual getting the fame."

For 50's part, he feels his continually growing success "makes me fit in because both Eminem and Dre are bosses. I fit into that and I'm working my way to being respected as if I'm equivalent to Eminem and Dre...I'm happy...I ain't never imagine that."

Consistent with his parent company's monopolistic business plan, 50 Cent has no intention of slowing down in 2005 following the March release of "St. Valentine's Day Massacre...(Then) I go to shoot my movie in April for 10 weeks…(In terms of the movie), we tailor-fit it. It's loosely based on my life story. It's difficult…Think about your life story. No matter how your life is, it's difficult to pick out what points you need to put in a two-hour film. You have to take your overall situation and create a story that kind of describes the best description of your life. You don't want to put people to sleep. The script is so good. I'm excited. For me it's more of a challenge than the music. I've already proven to myself that my ideas work….Then I have the soundtrack for the film, then Tony Yayo and Olivia's albums are being released, then Lloyd Banks and Young Buck's albums will be coming out in the fourth quarter alongside my video game I got with Universal for Bulletproof which is their answer to Grand Theft Auto. I got a book deal and a deal with Garcia Vitamin Water for Formula 50."

Still ever the hustler, 50 reasoned that "having this music, having Tony Yayo on deck and ready to go, following my album, after having Game sell 586,933 his first week, I'm anticipating selling even more than that my first week and then Yayo could possibly make more than that too, we're going uphill right now…Shortly after (my album's release in March), you'll see the first female solo artist of G-Unit, Olivia…I feel like I'm gonna have the biggest year in my career possibly this year."

Addressing the topic of longevity, 50 explained that "I've always wanted to be happy and in peace. It's not always an option. Where I'm from we meet aggression with aggression. The kid in the schoolyard that doesn't want to fight always leaves with a black eye. If you allow them to walk over you, you invite them to do it more. Then you're subject to something even worse than you just going into the beef to begin with. That's just the way it is. Would I like not to have beef? Yeah. I'd like to just make music. Their beef is I make music better than them at this point."

"Maybe it'll decrease with time. Maybe when I retire. I have no intention of retiring. I'd like to make music until I can't make music anymore. Ain't gonna be no 50 Cent like Jay-Z retiring. I'm like LL… I'm going to be here until no one shows up. I love it too much." With mentors behind him like Eminem and Dr. Dre, both of whom have achieved the status of cultural icon, maintained their own artistic success commercially and critically, and in the same time, built respective business empires, 50 Cent looks as a student to Dre and Em continually as he makes his own rise in the latter categories, explaining that "I learned to be more patient (from Eminem and Dr. Dre). I always want to do as much as I can."

"They're more perfectionists. Sometimes over-perfectionists. When you get like that, out of habit you start to second, third and fourth guess what you thinking. For me, it's like I get it and I go, this is right. That's it. Let's go. I've been able to have success doing that. When I start second guessing myself I think I'm ruining it. It's not organic anymore, not natural. I can't say lines like, 'I love you like a fat kid loves cake' when I'm dead serious. I've got to be enjoying myself or I won't come up with it, creatively… People have disliked me since I can remember."

"It's just more people like me now than people who dislike me. More people know of me. Everyone's a judge…everyone's a critic. Everybody who bought a CD can criticize me. Now when people say I don't like 50 Cent they don't know me enough to not like me. Say you don't like the music. Say it's too aggressive. I break it down for them the way it is, the way I came up. When I make a record and I think I can't make a better record, I'll stop…That's the significance when Jay-Z says, 'What More Can I Say'."

Of course, 50 had much more to say, not just on his new album, but regarding his own future as he—through his success—has gained new perspective from the top of the mountain looking back down at all he's overcome in the course of his remarkable career thus far in the game. As fans, we've just seen the periphery of his ambition, because 50 is realizing his own potential in real time with his listeners. What we can expect from 50 Cent in the future depends on what his own expectations are for success in the rap game, and beyond.

First, 50 feels he still has enemies out there to defeat before he's truly unified the hip hop title belts, explaining that "I was competitive in the ring and hip-hop is competitive too…In so many ways they're similar. I think rappers condition themselves like boxers, so they all kind of feel like they're the champ. And if you fall in the position where you're actually the champ at the time, everyone else feels like you're their target. That's me now — I'm the heavyweight champ…I understand exactly why I get the envy and the jealousy I get, particularly in New York City…My last LP sold more than everyone that's released an album. Add them all up together and it ain't 11 million…I think (my enemies) have mistaken me…Their actions come from their interaction with the guy in this spot before me, Jay-Z."

"I think Jay-Z, he doesn't mind them saying things and doing what they doing 'cause he's looking at them like 'bum ass niggas.' So he don't say nothing to them because he feels they're beneath him. But I got the time and energy to ruin what is left of their careers…Its cool, this is what I'm used to…Its actually a comfort zone for me to have issues…I understand that Nas…he's watched his window of opportunity open and close in front of him and now he's a little bitter…Fat Joe and Jadakiss, come on, man. They don't even count…The difference is, it's not music beef (what I got going on with Murder Inc.)…It comes from the street, and that don't die. That stays the same…I ain't gonna let up off of them until their homes are in foreclosure…Till it's really that bad…For me, if you begin to destroy, you should destroy completely. They already went too far."

"Like right now at this particular point, if I let off of Murder Inc., they'll linger for a little bit and people will start to feel like it's OK to start to like them. They get back in position, then guess what? They want to fight again. Now, they're like, 'Oh, peace treaty, wave a white flag, everybody please get up off us. This kid is killing us.' Now that makes sense for them to do it at this point. But you let them get back on their feet and they gonna wanna fight again…If I sell one record under what I sold on my first album, in my head that's a failure…(On The Massacre), I gave them all the stuff I missed…I didn't give them everything (on Get Rich or Die Tryin'). It was just one album, its not alot, man."

"In my head, I still feel like I'm going uphill. I don't feel that I have peaked, at all. I don't feel like I have made my best record. I got so much ahead of me that I can't look at my accomplishments and be like 'That's it.'… "I make more money outside the record industry…I generate opportunities with my music…This is going to be my year."

Even as he raps to further secure his legacy as hip hop's next icon, 50 Cent also seems focused on expanding his empire into the outward expanses of entrepreneurialism now available to him, thanks in part to the blueprint invented by hip-hop mogul forefathers like Russell Simmons, Suge Knight and Sean 'P-Diddy' Combs, inherited and reinvented by Master P, Jay-Z and Damon Dash, and currently—in its third generation—being plied by the likes of Eminem, Dr. Dre and 50 Cent in its most refined and precise application.

50 Cent is taking aggressive advantage of the capital his initial success in 2003 earned him, seeking to pave new roads with his own stable of artists, and by breeding new superstars under the G-Unit brand, become a household name in hip-hop for generations to come. With personal net earnings for 2003/2004 topping the $50 Million mark and a # 1 debut on March 8th, 2005 for his sophomore album with a first-week soundscan tally of 1.14 million and counting, Curtis Jackson, a.k.a. 50 Cent is well on his way.

Rolling Stone Magazine, in a glowing 4-star review, raved that "50 Cent is the most likable rapper ever to need a bulletproof vest. Like his Kevlar-wearing predecessor and idol, Tupac Shakur, 50 has charisma up the muzzle-hole. But where Tupac could be manic and unpredictable, 50 is cool and easy to be around—you get the sense that if he weren't so busy getting shot, stabbed and selling millions of albums, he would be an enormously successful fraternity president or restaurateur. 50's bullet-riddled resume provides cover for the fact that he's a major piece of hip-hop beefcake. He works that angle more than ever on 'The Massacre,' the follow-up to 2003's 'Get Rich or Die Tryin'….50 is so entertaining that you don't mind hearing him wallow in Fat City (usually the very place where these kinds of megahit follow-ups hit the shoals)."

"On "Piggy Bank," he gloats hilariously about how well he's doing, thanks to his G Unit soldiers Lloyd Banks, Young Buck and the Game: "Banks' shit sells/Buck's shit sells/Game's shit sells/I'm rich as — hell."…50 almost never lets you see him sweat—he wants you to believe that he could be doing something else, like being a drug kingpin; rhyming is just something he happens to be good at. Don't believe him: He works to vary his flow on Massacre…For someone as prolific as 50—he shares Tupac's work habits, recording more than sixty tracks for this album—he's also very efficient…As always, 50's secret weapon is his singing voice—the deceptively amateur-sounding tenor croon that he deploys on almost every chorus here."

"50 knows perfectly the limitations of his voice—he stays within his register and more than makes up in personality what he lacks in technique…Unlike many rappers who sing off-key with perverse joy, 50 shows a jazzy touch when he sings the title hook to 'God Gave Me Style.'…You are required to forgive 50's shortcomings—namely his egomania and apparent lack of a conscience. Most rappers (like, say, Jay-Z) hold out the illusion that, underneath all the tough talk, they're basically good guys; with 50, you're not so sure."

"Whenever he bemoans the violence of the streets, it's never because he hates what crime and poverty have done to his friends, the kids, his city or his people—it's because he's worried about his own skin. Or maybe, on a very empathetic day, his grandmother… The most empathetic track on The Massacre, 'A Baltimore Love Thing,' is also its most ambitious. Over slow-grooving, flute-driven funk, the supposed former drug dealer assumes the voice of heroin itself, speaking directly to a female addict. 'We have a bond that cannot be broken…Promise me you'll come and see me/Even if it means you'll have to sell your momma's TV.' But it isn't just a drug metaphor; it covers the relationship a lot of fans have with 50 himself. Yes, I'm a bad habit, he's saying, but try and stop listening. Why can't you? 'God gave me style…It ain't my fault."

That same week, 50 Cent broke another record by holding three of the top five slots on the Billboard Hot 100 singles chart with 'Candy Shop' at No. 1, 'How We Do,' his collaboration with The Game, at No. 4, and 'Disco Inferno' at No. 5. The only downside of 50's stellar week was a surprise-beef that erupted-predictably in that involved 50 Cent, more surprising that his overnight rival was former G-Unit sensation The Game. As MTV.com reported, "a 24-year-old man who police have identified as Kevin Reed of Compton, California, was hospitalized after a shooting outside the offices of New York radio station Hot 97 on Monday night."

"Although police have not confirmed many details, a source close to the investigation said the incident occurred at around the time 50 Cent was making an appearance at the radio station to announce that the Game had been booted from the G-Unit. Police said Reed is expected to recover. According to the source, Game, who had been a guest on the station earlier in the evening, apparently returned to Hot 97's offices accompanied by an undisclosed number of men and tried to get into the building.

"At around the same time, 50 Cent's interview was audibly interrupted, some conferring occurred, and the interview ended abruptly. Game and company were not allowed into the building and subsequently began quarreling with a group of individuals who were leaving Hot 97. The altercation led to Reed being shot at least once in the left leg. He was rushed to St. Vincent's Hospital."

"Police have confirmed that Reed was struck just outside the building. However, contrary to some reports that have surfaced, police say the man was probably not a member of 50 Cent's entourage, but they are still investigating. Police reported that 50 himself was not involved in the dispute. There were also shots fired outside the office of Violator Management — the company that manages 50 Cent, Busta Rhymes, Tweet and Missy Elliott— on Monday night, but no one was injured, according to police."

"There are no suspects as of yet in either shooting. On the radio Monday night, 50—accompanied by G-Unit members Tony Yayo, Lloyd Banks and Olivia—told Funkmaster Flex that the Game was being excommunicated from the G-Unit because he felt the West Coast MC was disloyal. 50 told Flex he was disappointed with comments Game made on the station Saturday night, when Game revealed he would not be getting involved in the beefs 50 is stirring up with 'Piggy Bank.'"

"According to Flex, Game even said he was going to do a song with Nas. 'He's gone,' 50 scoffed. 'He might as well make the record.' 50 also said Game should stop saying 'G-Unit.' 'He thinks he's doing me a favor when he says that.' During his conversation with Flex, 50 claimed Interscope was going to drop the Game until 50 stepped in and got involved with The Documentary. 50 also insisted that he's making more money off The Documentary than Game is, and that he wrote more choruses than he's credited for."

"Game was on Hot 97 earlier in the evening, talking to host Angie Martinez. When listeners called in to ask about his and 50's problems, Game simply said he was going to continue to make 'good music.' Two nights prior, Game had said on-air that he and 50 did not have to be friends as long as they worked toward that same common goal: making good music. 50 Cent made an appearance on MTV's 'TRL' Friday to promote his The Massacre LP and was questioned by the show's hosts about the shooting that took place Monday at radio station Hot 97. 'I didn't get to see very much,' he said, pointing out that he was on the air at the time. 'I think it's unfortunate those situations take place.' 50 said the public shouldn't be too concerned about the threat of violence between him and the people he's been squaring off against in the press and on his dis record "Piggy Bank". 50 said hip-hop is competitive and "they should expect artists to go at each other through the music."… Appearing with G-Unit member Olivia on BET's '106 & Park,' he compared himself to a boxing champ whose title everybody wants. "Where I'm from is aggressive…I was taught to be aggressive, so I say these things…A lot of things you hear out there is being said for shock value and not really as serious as people make it out to be."

"Claiming to be unimpressed with the responses of the MCs he targeted, he continued, saying, 'The media gets it and they try to do what they can do with it to make money off of it and make it look as bad as possible. But hip-hop has always been competitive, and they should always look forward to us getting back and forth with words.' " Within the week however, 50 and The Game—perhaps in the interest of being contractually obligated team players—called a truce.

As MTV.com news reported, "Apparently the Game and 50 Cent have put aside their issues. The two publicly buried the hatchet on Wednesday at a joint press conference in Harlem…Although the Game and 50 barely made eye contact or spoke to each other, they did shake hands and pose for photographers, and 50 even put his arm around Game. The rappers also donated a combined $253,500 to the Boys Choir of Harlem.…50 was the first to address the Schomburg Center crowd, which included the Reverend Run and Russell Simmons. 'In the shadow of the untimely death of Biggie—today marks the anniversary of his death—we're here today to show people we can rise above even the most difficult circumstances and together we can put negativity behind us,' he said as Game stood off to the side behind him with virtually no expression on his face..."

"When Game took the podium, he apologized to the fans, the radio stations and their label on behalf of himself and 50 for their beef consuming the headlines. 'I'm almost ashamed to have participated in the things that went on the past couple of weeks...I'm here, I'm apologetic...On behalf of myself and 50, we're making a statement that is a lot louder than just two voices...We're showing that you can control your destiny—not only your destiny, your future...Not only am I gonna control mine, I'm gonna control mine in a productive and positive way... I see this as a real opportunity to show the power of our community...50 and I are proving that real situations and real problems can be solved with real talk."

"This can also be seen as a big step for my organization, Black Wall Street, in terms of making a difference. Maybe we can help save some lives...the way rap music saved mine.' Game said that when he heard 50 was donating money to the choir, he wanted to be down, adding that 50 will be also giving money to one of the charities he is involved in...Boys Choir of Harlem founder Dr. Walter Turnbull was on hand to accept two checks for his organization—one from 50 for $150,000 dollars, and one from Game for $103,500...The choir was started in 1968 and has become world renowned, appearing last year on Kanye West's hit 'Jesus Walks.' The organization also has a school, the Choir Academy of Harlem, and has fallen on hard times of late and is in need of funds."

"Turnbull said 50 and Game are among the first to step to the plate with aid...Game and 50 have also pledged unspecified dollars to the Compton Unified School District's music program and have other plans in the works to help the community. 'I'm launching a new foundation, the G-Unity Foundation Inc., to help people overcome obstacles and make a change for the better in their lives...to help them overcome their situations...I realized that if I'm going to be effective at that, I have to overcome some of my own. Game and I need to set an example in the community." 50—behind the scenes—seemed to have a much simpler logic in mind when he drew a truce with Game, reasoning that "Nah, I'm cool with him…We cool, we work, we made the records that they hear in my house. If I didn't like him, they would know. Ultimately, the papers is signed, so whether I liked him or not I would still be paid."

In the end, for all his grand accomplishments and plans for the future, 50 seems determined to go out of the rap game the same way he'd come in—as his own man, such that according to 50 Cent, "(Five years ago), I really didn't (think I would be here.) I created a plan. I think everyone should have one. A five-year plan that you may shorten. You make short-term goals leading to your long-term goals. What happened to me was the success of Get Rich Or Die Tryin' sped up my five-year plan to a frame of about six months. I was able to maneuver everything else after those opportunities were provided for me because I had thought ahead. It wasn't like I was stuck. My first album, I said G-Unit, we in here. I was anticipating developing G-Unit into a record company. A lot of people view us as a group and as I begin to diversify the kind of music that comes from our camp, they'll start to appreciate us more as a company…I'm not ever gonna retire. I'm only dropping my second album, I'm so early in my career. Because my first album was such a big success, people start asking 'when you're gonna retire?' But I'm not even thinking about that, I'm more in the mind frame 'when do I come out again…'"

"I love Dre, but if he's confused with what direction he wants to go in after this, my next album will have the same 20 cuts this album has on it, but it will be sold as a double-CD. It will fulfill my requirements with Interscope Records. It will be the end of my Shady/Aftermath (deal) and I will move forward in my career as a Shady/G-Unit artist…Immortality (keeps me) level-headed. You've got an artist around you (in Eminem) that sold eighteen million records while you did eleven. And he's had the consistency to have projects go back to back. I'm surrounded by a lot of things that keep me grounded and keep me hungry, and wanting to do well."

"I also wanted to develop my record company…I'll be in the same games/same business, five years from now I probably would have released another album. It took me two years to come back with this one so if everything goes according to schedule I just went through I will have two more solo albums out because this is a beginning of my career I think people will look at the success and I've had and expect me to sell one or two more albums and I'm going to retire…I don't even see retirement right now."

50 Cent Chart History/Discography:

Albums:

▼ "Get Rich or Die Tryin"
Released: February, 2003
Label: Shady/Aftermath/Interscope Records
US: 6x Platinum
Billboard peak: # 1 (for 6 weeks)

▼ "50 Cent: The New Breed" (CD & DVD)
Released: April, 2003
Label: Shady/Aftermath/Interscope Records
US: Platinum
Billboard peak: # 2

▼ "Power of the Dollar"
Label: Trackmasters/Columbia/Sony Records
Original Release Date: September 12, 2000 (Never originally
released due to shooting), re-released March, 2003.

Bootlegs/Mixtapes:

▼ 50 Cent/G-Unit—Guess Who's Back
Release Date: May 21, 2002

▼ 50 Cent/G-Unit
Release Date: June 1, 2002

▼ 50 Cent—No Fear, No Mercy
Release Date: June 1, 2002

▼ 50 Cent/G-Unit—God's Plan
Release Date: August 1, 2002

Singles:

▼ "In Da Club"—# 1 for 4 weeks on the Billboard Top 100 Singles Chart, # 1 on the Billboard Hot R&B Singles Chart for 6 weeks

▼ "21 Questions", Featuring Nate Dogg—# 1 for 4 weeks on the Billboard Top 100 Singles Chart, # 1 on the Billboard R&B Singles Chart for 7 weeks

▼ "P.I.M.P."—Top 10 Single on the Billboard Top 100 Singles Chart and Hot R&B Singles Chart

Awards:

▼ 2003 BET Awards: 2 awards won for Best Male Hip-Hop Artist and Best New Artist.

▼ 2003 MTV Video Music Awards: 2 awards won for Best Rap Video and Best New Artist, and was nominated for Video of the Year, Best Male Video, and Viewer's Choice.

▼ 2003 World Music Awards: 5 awards won including Best Artist 2003, Best Pop Male Artist, Best R&B Artist, Best Rap/Hip-Hop Artist, and Best New Artist.

▼ 2003 Source Awards: 2 awards won for Album of the Year (Get Rich or Die Tryin') and Single of the Year, Male (In Da Club).

▼ 2003 Radio Music Awards—1 award won for Artist of the Year —Hip-Hop Radio.

▼ 2003 American Music Awards—2 awards won for Favorite Rap/Hip-Hop Album and Favorite Rap/Hip-Hop Male Artist and was nominated for the Fan's Choice Award.

▼ 2003 Vibe Awards—3 awards won for Artist of the Year, Dopest Album, and Hottest Hook.

▼ 2004 Grammy Awards—nominated for 5 Grammy Awards including Best Rap Performance by a Duo or Group, Best

Male Rap Solo Performance, Best Rap Album, Best New Artist, and Best Rap Song.

Overall Singles/Albums/Awards History Between 2002 and 2004:

(Source: Rockonthenet.com)

2002:

▼ 8 Mile Soundtrack, 4 X Platinum, Single: Wanksta, Number 1 MTV Video

2003:

▼ Number 2 Singles Artist of the Year (source: The ARC Weekly Top 40 Charts, 2003)

February

▼ 50 Cent topped the Billboard Hot Rap Singles chart, the R&B/Hip-Hop Singles & Tracks chart for 9 weeks, and the R&B/Hip-Hop Airplay chart for 9 weeks with "In Da Club."

▼ 50 Cent released 'Get Rich or Die Tryin'. The LP includes help from Eminem, Nate Dogg, and Dr. Dre.

▼ 50 Cent hit the Top 40 with "In Da Club"

▼ Get Rich or Die Tryin' topped the Billboard 200 Album chart for 6 weeks and Hot R&B/Hip-Hop Albums chart for 8 weeks selling over 872,000 copies in its first week of release in the US —a shorter release week than usual after the release date was pushed up to thwart bootlegging and downloading.

▼ Get HGGet Rich or Die Tryin' topped the LP charts in Canada.

▼ 50 Cent can be heard on the soundtrack for 'Cradle 2 the Grave' with 'Follow Me Gangster.'

March

▼ 50 Cent topped the Billboard Hot 100 singles chart for 9 weeks and the Hot 100 Airplay chart for 9 weeks with "In Da Club."

▼ 50 Cent hit the Top 10 with "In Da Club" and then #1 for 4 weeks.

▼ "In Da Club" broke a *Billboard* magazine record as the 'most listened-to' song in radio history within a week.

▼ 'Get Rich or Die Tryin' was certified 4x platinum.

▼ 50 Cent helped out Lil' Kim on the track "Magic Stick" for her LP, 'La Bella Mafia.'

April

▼ 50 Cent: The New Breed (CD & DVD) was released.

▼ 50 Cent appeared on the cover of *Rolling Stone Magazine*.

▼ 50 Cent hit the Top 40 with Nate Dogg with "21 Questions."

▼ 50 Cent topped the Billboard Hot R&B/Hip-Hop Singles & Tracks chart, and R&B/Hip-Hop Airplay chart for 8 weeks with "21 Question."

▼ 50 Cent topped the Canadian singles charts with "In Da Club."

May

▼ 50 Cent performed on Saturday Night Live.

▼ 50 Cent: The New Breed topped the Billboard R&B/ Hip-Hop chart for a week.

▼ 50 Cent: The New Breed topped the Billboard Top Music Videos chart.

▼ 50 Cent topped the Billboard Hot 100 singles chart for 4 weeks, the Hot 100 Airplay chart for 5 weeks, the Hot R&B/ Hip-Hop Singles chart for 7 weeks, the Hot R&B/Hip-Hop Singles Sales chart for a week, and Hot Rap Tracks chart for 7 weeks with "21 Questions."

June

▼ 50 Cent hit the Top 10 with Nate Dogg with "21 Questions."

▼ 50 Cent and Jay-Z will start touring together as part of the 'Rock The Mic Tour' kicking off in June in Connecticut.

▼ 50 Cent hit the Top 40 helping out Lil' Kim with "Magic Stick" from her LP 'La Bella Mafia'.

▼ 50 Cent topped the Billboard Rap Singles chart for 5 weeks and Hot R&B/Hip-Hop Airplay chart for a week by helping out Lil' Kim with "Magic Stick."

▼ 50 Cent won 2 BET Awards for Best New Artist and Best Male Hip-Hop Artist.

▼ 'Get Rich or Die Tryin' was certified 5x platinum.

July

▼ 50 Cent topped the Billboard Hot 100 Airplay chart for a week helping out Lil' Kim with "Magic Stick".

▼ 50 Cent could be heard on the Bad Boys 2 Soundtrack with the track "Realest Niggaz."

▼ 50 Cent hit the Top 40 with "P.I.M.P."

▼ 50 Cent hit the Top 10 helping out Lil' Kim with "Magic Stick".

August

▼ 50 Cent's video for "In Da Club" won 2 MTV Video Music Awards for Best Rap Video and Best New Artist, and was nominated for Video of the Year, Best Male Video, and Viewer's Choice. 50 Cent also performed at the ceremony.

▼ 50 Cent topped the Billboard Hot Rap Tracks chart for 2 weeks with "P.I.M.P."

▼ 50 Cent could be heard on Mary J. Blige's LP, "Love & Life", on the track "Let Me Be The 1."

October

▼ 50 Cent hit the Top 10 with "P.I.M.P."

▼ 50 Cent won 5 World Music Awards including Best Artist 2003, Best Pop Male Artist, Best R&B Artist, Best Rap/Hip-Hop Artist, and Best New Artist.

▼ 50 Cent took home 2 Source Awards for Album of the Year 'Get Rich or Die Tryin' and Single of the Year, Male "In Da Club".

▼ 50 Cent won a Radio Music Awards for Artist of the Year —Hip-Hop Radio.

November

▼ 50 Cent was featured on the "Tupac: Resurrection" Soundtrack on the track "The Realist Killaz" with 2Pac.

▼ 50 Cent's G-Unit released "Beg For Mercy".

▼ 50 Cent won 2 American Music Awards for Favorite Rap/Hip-Hop Album and Favorite Rap/Hip-Hop Male Artist and was nominated for the Fan's Choice Award.

▼ 50 Cent won 3 Vibe Awards including Artist of the Year, Dopest Album, and Hottest Hook "In Da Club."

December

▼ 'Get Rich or Die Tryin' was certified 6x platinum.

▼ 50 Cent had the Top Music Video Sales title of the year with 'The New Breed.'

▼ Readers of *Rolling Stone Magazine* named 50 Cent as the Best New Artist.

▼ 50 Cent topped the Billboard Year End Artists as the Top Pop Artist (singles & albums), Top Pop Artist—Male (singles & albums), Top Billboard 200 Album, Top Billboard 200 Album Artist—Male, Top Hot 100 Singles Artist, Top Hot 100 Singles Artist—Male, Top R&B/Hip-Hop Artist (singles & albums), Top R&B/Hip-Hop Artist —Male (singles & albums), Top R&B/Hip-Hop Album Artist, Top R&B/Hip-Hop Album Artist —Male, Top Hot R&B/Hip-Hop Singles & Tracks

Artist, Top Hot R&B/Hip-Hop Singles & Tracks Artist —Male, Top Hot Rhythmic Top 40 Artist, Top Hot Rap Artist —and with the Top Billboard 200 Album Artist and Top R&B/Hip-Hop Album 'Get Rich or Die Tryin', and the Top Hot 100 Singles & Tracks, Top Hot 100 Airplay Track, Top Hot R&B/Hip-Hop Singles & Tracks, Top Hot R&B/ Hip-Hop Airplay, and Top Hot Rap Single 'In Da Club.'

▼ 50 Cent had the biggest selling LP of the year —'Get Rich or Die Tryin' —which sold over 6.5 million copies during the year in the US.

2004:

February

▼ 50 Cent was nominated for **5 Grammy Awards** including Best Rap Performance by a Duo or Group, Best Male Rap Solo Performance, Best Rap Album, Best New Artist, and Best Rap Song (songwriter).

▼ 50 Cent won a Brit Award for Best International Breakthrough Artists.

August

▼ The video for "P.I.M.P." was nominated for a MTV Video Music Award including Best Rap Video.

▼ 50 Cent will make an animated appearance on the FOX series The Simpsons next season.

▼ 50 Cent's next LP was originally scheduled for a February, 2004 release and then pushed back until June, will now be released in October

About the Author

Jake Brown resides in Nashville, Tennessee and is President of Versailles Records. An avid writer he has penned several books, including the best-sellers: *SUGE KNIGHT – The Rise, Fall & Rise of Death Row Records; Your Body's Calling Me: The Life and Times of Robert "R" Kelly –*  *Music Love, Sex & Money and READY to Die: The Story of Biggie —Notorious B.I.G. Upcoming titles on Colossus Books are: JAY-Z....AND the Roc-A-Fella Dynasty and Tupac SHAKUR (2-PAC) IN the Studio: The Studio Years (1987-1996).*

ORDER FORM

WWW.AMBERBOOKS.COM

Fax Orders: 480-283-0991   Telephone Orders: 480-460-1660

Postal Orders: Send Checks & Money Orders to:
>   Amber Books
>   1334 E. Chandler Blvd., Suite 5-D67, Phoenix, AZ 85048

Online Orders: E-mail: Amberbk@aol.com

_____ *50 Cent: No Holds Barred*, ISBN#: 0-9767735-2-X, $16.95

_____ *Jay-Z…and the Roc-A-Fella Dynasty*, ISBN#: 0-9749779-1-8, $16.95

_____ *Your Body's Calling Me: The Life & Times of "Robert" R. Kelly*, ISBN#: 0-9727519-5-52, $16.95

_____ *Ready to Die: Notorious B.I.G.*, ISBN#: 0-9749779-3-4, $16.95

_____ *Suge Knight: The Rise, Fall, and Rise of Death Row Records*, ISBN#: 0-9702224-7-5, $21.95

_____ *Aaliyah—An R&B Princess in Words and Pictures* , ISBN#: 0-9702224-3-2, $10.95

_____ *You Forgot About Dre: Dr. Dre & Eminem*, ISBN#: 0-9702224-9-1, $10.95

_____ *Divas of the New Millenium*, ISBN#: 0-9749779-6-9, $16.95

_____ *Michael Jackson: The King of Pop*, ISBN#: 0-9749779-0-X, $29.95

_____ *The House that Jack Built (Hal Jackson Story)*, ISBN#: 0-9727519-4-7, $16.95

Name:_____

Company Name:_____

Address:_____

City:_____State:_____Zip:_____

Telephone: (____) _____E-mail:_____

For Bulk Rates Call: **480-460-1660**   ## ORDER NOW

50 Cent: No Holds Barred,	$16.95	❑ Check ❑ Money Order ❑ Cashiers Check
Jay-Z…and the Roc-A-Fella Dynasty	$16.95	❑ Credit Card: ❑ MC ❑ Visa ❑ Amex ❑
Your Body's Calling Me:	$16.95	Discover
Ready to Die: Notorious B.I.G.,	$16.95	
Suge Knight:	$21.95	
Aaliyah—An R&B Princess	$10.95	CC#_____
Dr. Dre & Eminem	$10.95	
Divas of the New Millenium,	$16.95	Expiration Date:_____
Michael Jackson: The King of Pop	$29.95	**Payable to:**
The House that Jack Built	$16.95	Amber Books

Payable to:
>   Amber Books
>   1334 E. Chandler Blvd., Suite 5-D67
>   Phoenix, AZ 85048

Shipping: $5.00 per book. Allow 7 days for delivery.

Sales Tax: Add 7.05% to books shipped to Arizona addresses.

Total enclosed: $_____